this tracker-planner belongs to:

____

Chronic Illness Tracker-Planner: Ostomy Edition

Published by Glory Box Press
British Columbia, Canada.
gloryboxpress@gmail.com

First edition, 2021

ISBN 978-1-989884-35-5

Cover design, interior design, and formatting by Glory Box Press
Editing by Glory Box Press

how to use
your tracker-
planner

DAILY CHECK-IN, PLANNER, AND TRACKER

DATE: M T (W) T F S S Month: january Day: 17

wake time: 6:00 a.m. bedtime: 10:00 p.m.

hours slept: 8

how rested i feel:

micro goals	priorities	optional
mail package finish chapter 7	litter box!	clean closet save the world

medication tracker	6am-10 am	10am-2pm	2pm-6pm	6pm-10pm	overnight
	✓	✓			
	additional:	stelara			

meal tracker

time	what i ate	how i felt
7am	orange, Boost	some nausea, but not bad

caffeine	III
alcohol	I
nicotine/vape	–

physical activity

swimming, 45 min.

ostomy output tracker

bag changes	0									
bag empty/output	l s t	l s t	l s t	l s t	l s t	l s t	l s t	l s t	l s t	l s t
bag burp										

l = liquid output / s = semi-liquid/semi-thick / t = thick

symptom tracker

pain										
stress										
fatigue										
brain fog										
scale	1	2	3	4	5	6	7	8	9	10

pain triggers

depression / anxiety / stress / no meds/ poor sleep / lack of activity / weather / overdid it

pain type and location:

achy / burning / stabbing / cramping / shooting / heavy / sharp / weak / throbbing

triggers
(what made me happy, stressed etc.)

deadline (stress!)

chat w emily. (woot!)

good things that happened

beat the water temple level! I'M A BEAST

things that sucked

metho made me feel sick all day

self-care

unicorn bath bomb because i AM AWESOME!

1 hour of zelda

overall mood today:

chronic illness tracker-planner

ostomy edition

GLORY BOX PRESS

monthly planner

month: ____________

what i will do for self-care:

what i'm looking forward to most:

what i have to get through:

how i will cope:

what i want to accomplish this month:

appointment tracker

date	time	doctor	location	issue	outcome

current medications

name	dose	times per day/week/month	side effects	refill on:

new treatment/medication:

weekly planner

week of: ___________

what i will do for self-care:

what i'm looking forward to most:

what i have to get through:

how i will cope:

what i want to accomplish this week:

DAILY CHECK-IN, PLANNER, AND TRACKER

DATE: M T W T F S S Month: ___________ Day: ___________

today's intention

today's challenges

wake time: _______ a.m. bedtime: _______ p.m.

hours slept: _______

how rested i feel:

micro goals

priorities

optional

medication tracker	6am-10 am	10am-2pm	2pm-6pm	6pm-10pm	overnight
	additional:				

meal tracker

time	what i ate	how i felt

caffeine	
alcohol	
nicotine/vape	

physical activity

ostomy output tracker

bag changes										
bag empty/output	l s t	l s t	l s t	l s t	l s t	l s t	l s t	l s t	l s t	l s t
bag burp										

l = liquid output / s = semi-liquid/semi-thick / t = thick

symptom tracker

pain										
stress										
fatigue										
brain fog										
scale	1	2	3	4	5	6	7	8	9	10

pain triggers

depression / anxiety / stress / no meds/ poor sleep / lack of activity / weather / overdid it

pain type and location:

achy / burning / stabbing / cramping / shooting / heavy / sharp / weak / throbbing

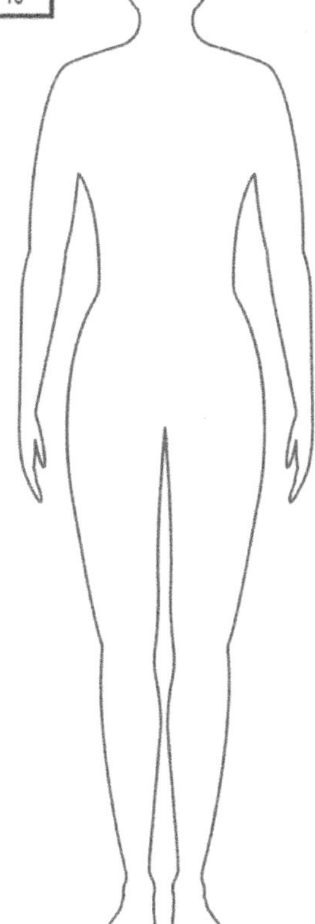

triggers (what made me happy, stressed etc.)	good things that happened	things that sucked

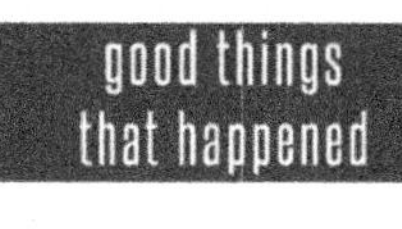

self-care

overall mood today:

DAILY CHECK-IN, PLANNER, AND TRACKER

DATE: M T W T F S S Month: __________ Day: __________

today's intention

today's challenges

wake time: ______ a.m. bedtime: ______ p.m.

hours slept: ______

how rested i feel:

micro goals	priorities	optional

medication tracker	6am-10 am	10am-2pm	2pm-6pm	6pm-10pm	overnight
	additional:				

meal tracker

time	what i ate	how i felt

caffeine	
alcohol	
nicotine/vape	

physical activity

ostomy output tracker

bag changes										
bag empty/output	l s t	l s t	l s t	l s t	l s t	l s t	l s t	l s t	l s t	l s t
bag burp										

l = liquid output / s = semi-liquid/semi-thick / t = thick

symptom tracker

pain										
stress										
fatigue										
brain fog										
scale	1	2	3	4	5	6	7	8	9	10

pain triggers

depression / anxiety / stress / no meds/ poor sleep / lack of activity / weather / overdid it

pain type and location:

achy / burning / stabbing / cramping / shooting / heavy / sharp / weak / throbbing

triggers
(what made me happy, stressed etc.)

good things that happened

things that sucked

self-care

DAILY CHECK-IN, PLANNER, AND TRACKER

DATE: M T W T F S S Month: __________ Day: __________

today's intention

today's challenges

wake time: ______ a.m. bedtime: ______ p.m.

hours slept: ______

how rested i feel:

micro goals	priorities	optional

medication tracker	6am-10 am	10am-2pm	2pm-6pm	6pm-10pm	overnight
	additional:				

meal tracker

time	what i ate	how i felt

caffeine	
alcohol	
nicotine/vape	

physical activity

ostomy output tracker

bag changes										
bag empty/output	l s t	l s t	l s t	l s t	l s t	l s t	l s t	l s t	l s t	l s t
bag burp										

l = liquid output / s = semi-liquid/semi-thick / t = thick

symptom tracker

pain										
stress										
fatigue										
brain fog										
scale	1	2	3	4	5	6	7	8	9	10

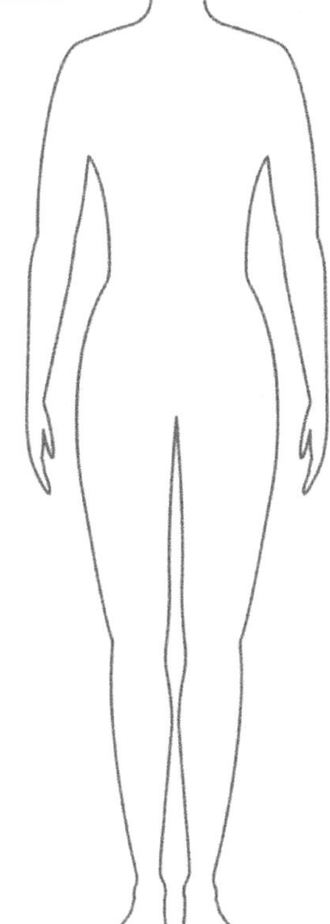

pain triggers

depression / anxiety / stress / no meds/ poor sleep / lack of activity / weather / overdid it

pain type and location:

achy / burning / stabbing / cramping / shooting / heavy / sharp / weak / throbbing

triggers (what made me happy, stressed etc.)	good things that happened	things that sucked

self-care

overall mood today:

DAILY CHECK-IN, PLANNER, AND TRACKER

DATE: M T W T F S S Month: __________ Day: __________

today's intention

today's challenges

wake time: ______ a.m. bedtime: ______ p.m.

hours slept: ______

how rested i feel:

micro goals

priorities

optional

medication tracker	6am-10 am	10am-2pm	2pm-6pm	6pm-10pm	overnight
	additional:				

meal tracker

time	what i ate	how i felt

caffeine	
alcohol	
nicotine/vape	

physical activity

ostomy output tracker

bag changes										
bag empty/output	l s t	l s t	l s t	l s t	l s t	l s t	l s t	l s t	l s t	l s t
bag burp										

l = liquid output / s = semi-liquid/semi-thick / t = thick

symptom tracker

pain										
stress										
fatigue										
brain fog										
scale	1	2	3	4	5	6	7	8	9	10

pain triggers

depression / anxiety / stress / no meds/ poor sleep / lack of activity / weather / overdid it

pain type and location:

achy / burning / stabbing / cramping / shooting / heavy / sharp / weak / throbbing

triggers
(what made me happy, stressed etc.)

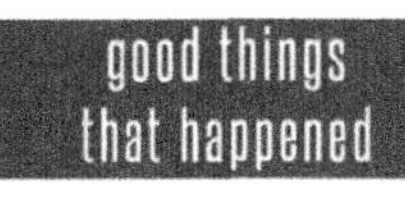

good things that happened

things that sucked

self-care

overall mood today:

DAILY CHECK-IN, PLANNER, AND TRACKER

DATE: M T W T F S S Month: ___________ Day: ___________

today's intention

today's challenges

wake time: ______ a.m. bedtime: ______ p.m.

hours slept: _______

how rested i feel:

micro goals	priorities	optional

medication tracker	6am-10 am	10am-2pm	2pm-6pm	6pm-10pm	overnight
	additional:				

meal tracker

time	what i ate	how i felt

caffeine	
alcohol	
nicotine/vape	

physical activity

ostomy output tracker

bag changes										
bag empty/output	l s t	l s t	l s t	l s t	l s t	l s t	l s t	l s t	l s t	l s t
bag burp										

l = liquid output / s = semi-liquid/semi-thick / t = thick

symptom tracker

pain										
stress										
fatigue										
brain fog										
scale	1	2	3	4	5	6	7	8	9	10

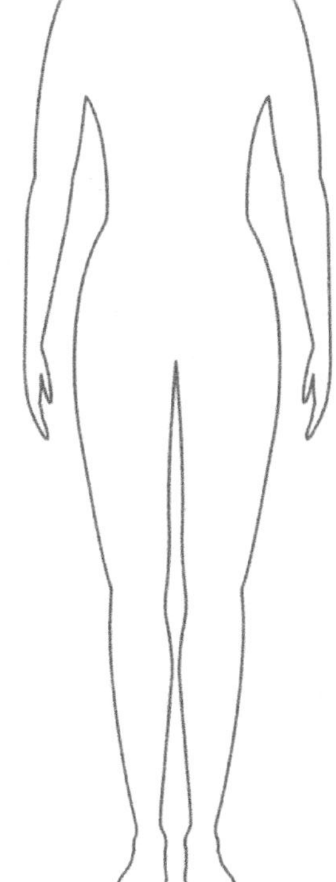

pain triggers

depression / anxiety / stress / no meds/ poor sleep / lack of activity / weather / overdid it

pain type and location:

achy / burning / stabbing / cramping / shooting / heavy / sharp / weak / throbbing

triggers (what made me happy, stressed etc.)	good things that happened	things that sucked

self-care

overall mood today:

DAILY CHECK-IN, PLANNER, AND TRACKER

DATE: M T W T F S S Month: __________ Day: __________

today's intention

today's challenges

wake time: ______ a.m. bedtime: ______ p.m.

hours slept: ______

how rested i feel:

micro goals

priorities

optional

medication tracker	6am-10 am	10am-2pm	2pm-6pm	6pm-10pm	overnight
	additional:				

meal tracker

time	what i ate	how i felt

caffeine	
alcohol	
nicotine/vape	

physical activity

ostomy output tracker

bag changes										
bag empty/output	l s t	l s t	l s t	l s t	l s t	l s t	l s t	l s t	l s t	l s t
bag burp										

l = liquid output / s = semi-liquid/semi-thick / t = thick

symptom tracker

pain										
stress										
fatigue										
brain fog										
scale	1	2	3	4	5	6	7	8	9	10

pain triggers

depression / anxiety / stress / no meds/ poor sleep / lack of activity / weather / overdid it

pain type and location:

achy / burning / stabbing / cramping / shooting / heavy / sharp / weak / throbbing

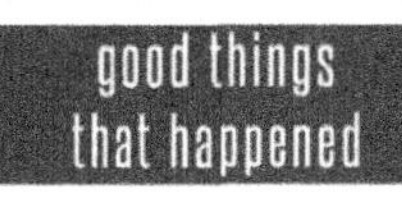

triggers
(what made me happy, stressed etc.)

good things that happened

things that sucked

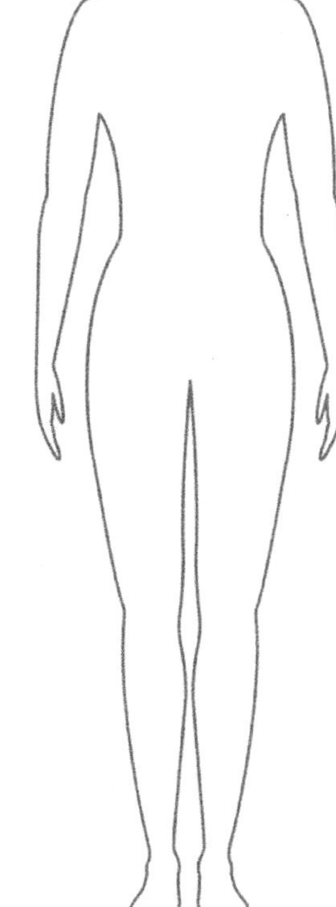

self-care

overall mood today:

DAILY CHECK-IN, PLANNER, AND TRACKER

DATE: M T W T F S S Month: __________ Day: __________

today's intention

today's challenges

wake time: ______ a.m. bedtime: ______ p.m.

hours slept: ______

how rested i feel:

😄 🙂 😕 ☹️ 😵

micro goals

priorities

optional

medication tracker	6am-10 am	10am-2pm	2pm-6pm	6pm-10pm	overnight
	additional:				

meal tracker

time	what i ate	how i felt

caffeine	
alcohol	
nicotine/vape	

physical activity

ostomy output tracker

bag changes										
bag empty/output	l s t	l s t	l s t	l s t	l s t	l s t	l s t	l s t	l s t	l s t
bag burp										

l = liquid output / s = semi-liquid/semi-thick / t = thick

symptom tracker

pain										
stress										
fatigue										
brain fog										
scale	1	2	3	4	5	6	7	8	9	10

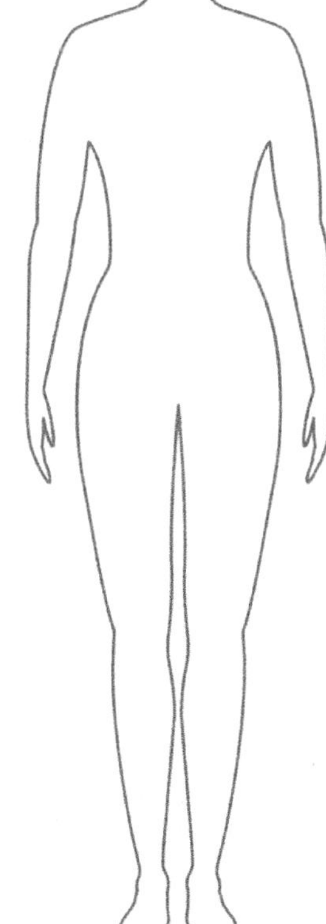

pain triggers

depression / anxiety / stress / no meds/ poor sleep / lack of activity / weather / overdid it

pain type and location:

achy / burning / stabbing / cramping / shooting / heavy / sharp / weak / throbbing

triggers
(what made me happy, stressed etc.)

good things that happened

things that sucked

self-care

overall mood today:

weekly review

week of: ____________________

my successes:

what i accepted:

what i let go:

what i did for self-care:

what was better this week:

what was worse this week:

pain summary:

medication/
care changes:

weekly planner

week of: ____________

what i will do for self-care:

what i'm looking forward to most:

what i have to get through:

how i will cope:

what i want to accomplish this week:

DAILY CHECK-IN, PLANNER, AND TRACKER

DATE: M T W T F S S Month: __________ Day: __________

today's intention

today's challenges

wake time: ______ a.m. bedtime: ______ p.m.

hours slept: ______

how rested i feel:

micro goals

priorities

optional

medication tracker	6am-10 am	10am-2pm	2pm-6pm	6pm-10pm	overnight
	additional:				

meal tracker

time	what i ate	how i felt

caffeine	
alcohol	
nicotine/vape	

physical activity

ostomy output tracker

bag changes										
bag empty/output	l s t	l s t	l s t	l s t	l s t	l s t	l s t	l s t	l s t	l s t
bag burp										

l = liquid output / s = semi-liquid/semi-thick / t = thick

symptom tracker

pain										
stress										
fatigue										
brain fog										
scale	1	2	3	4	5	6	7	8	9	10

pain triggers

depression / anxiety / stress / no meds/ poor sleep / lack of activity / weather / overdid it

pain type and location:

achy / burning / stabbing / cramping / shooting / heavy / sharp / weak / throbbing

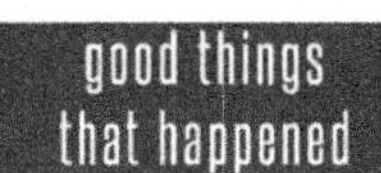

triggers
(what made me happy, stressed etc.)

good things that happened

things that sucked

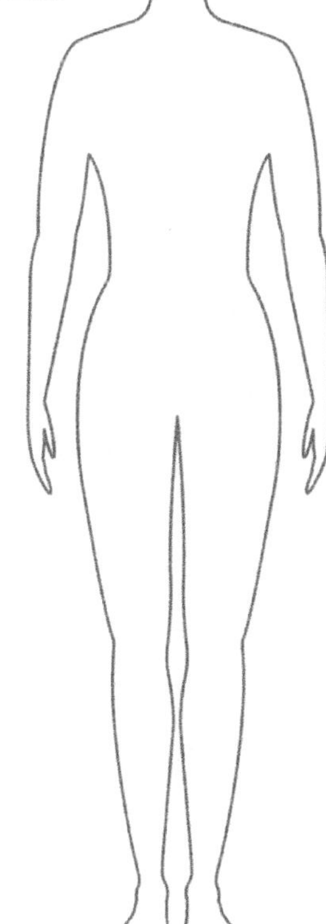

self-care

overall mood today:

DAILY CHECK-IN, PLANNER, AND TRACKER

DATE: M T W T F S S Month: __________ Day: __________

today's intention

today's challenges

wake time: ______ a.m. bedtime: ______ p.m.

hours slept: ______

how rested i feel:

micro goals	priorities	optional

medication tracker	6am-10 am	10am-2pm	2pm-6pm	6pm-10pm	overnight
	additional:				

meal tracker

time	what i ate	how i felt

caffeine	
alcohol	
nicotine/vape	

physical activity

ostomy output tracker

bag changes										
bag empty/output	l s t	l s t	l s t	l s t	l s t	l s t	l s t	l s t	l s t	l s t
bag burp										

l = liquid output / s = semi-liquid/semi-thick / t = thick

symptom tracker

pain										
stress										
fatigue										
brain fog										
scale	1	2	3	4	5	6	7	8	9	10

pain triggers

depression / anxiety / stress / no meds/ poor sleep / lack of activity / weather / overdid it

pain type and location:

achy / burning / stabbing / cramping / shooting / heavy / sharp / weak / throbbing

triggers
(what made me happy, stressed etc.)

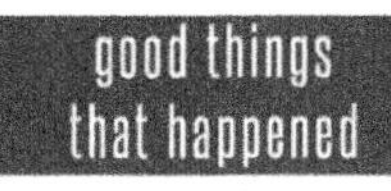

good things that happened

things that sucked

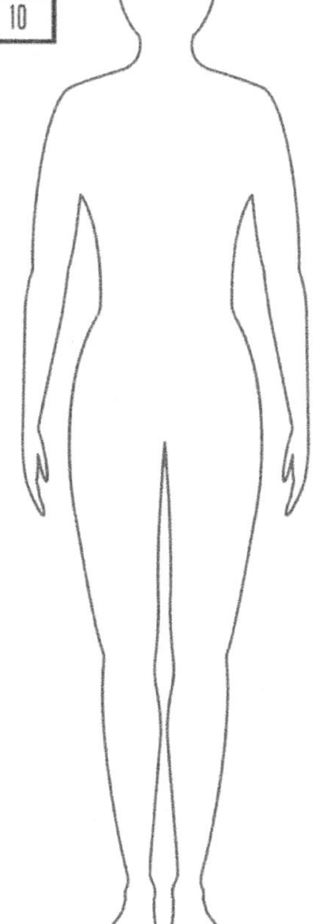

self-care

overall mood today:

DAILY CHECK-IN, PLANNER, AND TRACKER

DATE: M T W T F S S Month: __________ Day: __________

today's intention

today's challenges

wake time: ______ a.m. bedtime: ______ p.m.

hours slept: ______

how rested i feel:

micro goals	priorities	optional

medication tracker	6am-10 am	10am-2pm	2pm-6pm	6pm-10pm	overnight
	additional:				

meal tracker

time	what i ate	how i felt

caffeine	
alcohol	
nicotine/vape	

physical activity

ostomy output tracker

bag changes										
bag empty/output	l s t	l s t	l s t	l s t	l s t	l s t	l s t	l s t	l s t	l s t
bag burp										

l = liquid output / s = semi-liquid/semi-thick / t = thick

symptom tracker

pain										
stress										
fatigue										
brain fog										
scale	1	2	3	4	5	6	7	8	9	10

pain triggers

depression / anxiety / stress / no meds/ poor sleep / lack of activity / weather / overdid it

pain type and location:

achy / burning / stabbing / cramping / shooting / heavy / sharp / weak / throbbing

triggers
(what made me happy, stressed etc.)

good things that happened

things that sucked

self-care

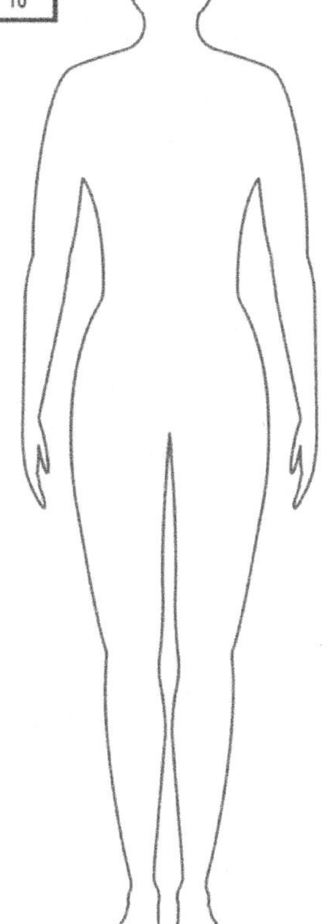

overall mood today:

DAILY CHECK-IN, PLANNER, AND TRACKER

DATE: M T W T F S S Month: __________ Day: __________

today's intention

today's challenges

wake time: ______ a.m. bedtime: ______ p.m.

hours slept: ______

how rested i feel:

micro goals

priorities

optional

medication tracker	6am-10 am	10am-2pm	2pm-6pm	6pm-10pm	overnight
	additional:				

meal tracker

time	what i ate	how i felt

caffeine	
alcohol	
nicotine/vape	

physical activity

ostomy output tracker

bag changes										
bag empty/output	l s t	l s t	l s t	l s t	l s t	l s t	l s t	l s t	l s t	l s t
bag burp										

l = liquid output / s = semi-liquid/semi-thick / t = thick

symptom tracker

pain										
stress										
fatigue										
brain fog										
scale	1	2	3	4	5	6	7	8	9	10

pain triggers

depression / anxiety / stress / no meds/ poor sleep / lack of activity / weather / overdid it

pain type and location:

achy / burning / stabbing / cramping / shooting / heavy / sharp / weak / throbbing

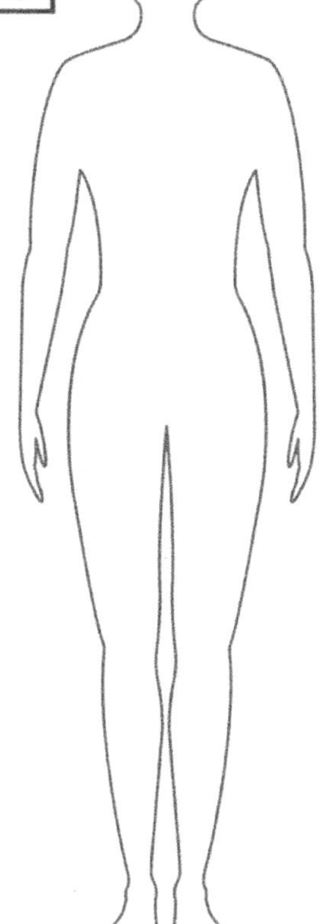

triggers
(what made me happy, stressed etc.)

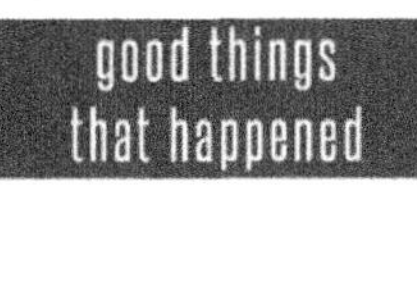

good things that happened

things that sucked

self-care

overall mood today:

DAILY CHECK-IN, PLANNER, AND TRACKER

DATE: M T W T F S S Month: __________ Day: __________

today's intention

today's challenges

wake time: ______ a.m. bedtime: ______ p.m.

hours slept: ______

how rested i feel:

micro goals

priorities

optional

medication tracker	6am-10 am	10am-2pm	2pm-6pm	6pm-10pm	overnight
	additional:				

meal tracker

time	what i ate	how i felt

caffeine	
alcohol	
nicotine/vape	

physical activity

ostomy output tracker

bag changes										
bag empty/output	l s t	l s t	l s t	l s t	l s t	l s t	l s t	l s t	l s t	l s t
bag burp										

l = liquid output / s = semi-liquid/semi-thick / t = thick

symptom tracker

pain										
stress										
fatigue										
brain fog										
scale	1	2	3	4	5	6	7	8	9	10

pain triggers

depression / anxiety / stress / no meds/ poor sleep / lack of activity / weather / overdid it

pain type and location:

achy / burning / stabbing / cramping / shooting / heavy / sharp / weak / throbbing

triggers
(what made me happy, stressed etc.)

good things that happened

things that sucked

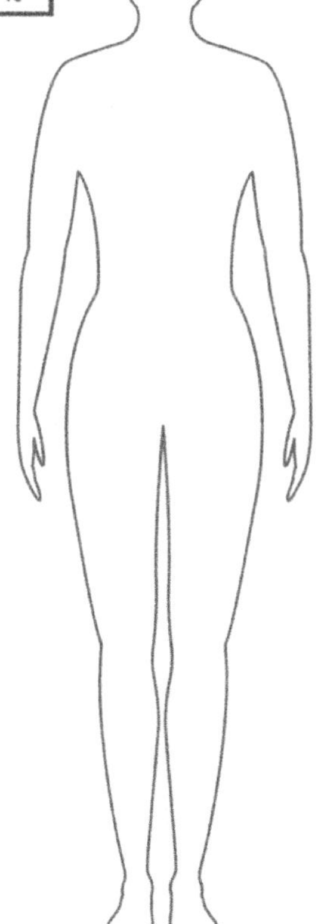

self-care

overall mood today:

DAILY CHECK-IN, PLANNER, AND TRACKER

DATE: M T W T F S S Month: ___________ Day: ___________

today's intention

today's challenges

wake time: ______ a.m. bedtime: ______ p.m.

hours slept: ______

how rested i feel:

micro goals

priorities

optional

medication tracker	6am-10 am	10am-2pm	2pm-6pm	6pm-10pm	overnight
	additional:				

meal tracker

time	what i ate	how i felt

caffeine	
alcohol	
nicotine/vape	

physical activity

ostomy output tracker

bag changes										
bag empty/output	l s t	l s t	l s t	l s t	l s t	l s t	l s t	l s t	l s t	l s t
bag burp										

l = liquid output / s = semi-liquid/semi-thick / t = thick

symptom tracker

pain										
stress										
fatigue										
brain fog										
scale	1	2	3	4	5	6	7	8	9	10

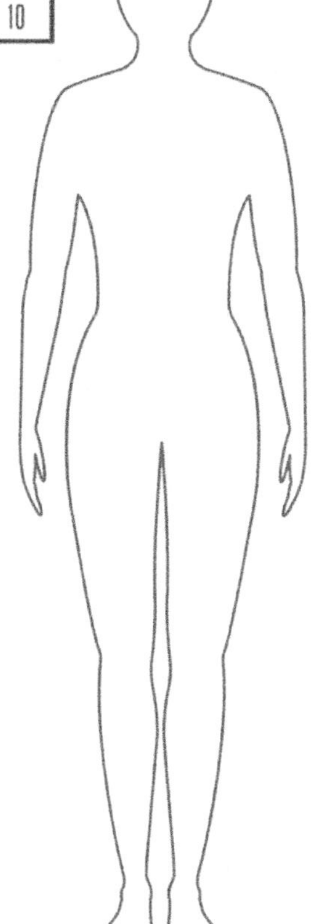

pain triggers

depression / anxiety / stress / no meds/ poor sleep / lack of activity / weather / overdid it

pain type and location:

achy / burning / stabbing / cramping / shooting / heavy / sharp / weak / throbbing

triggers
(what made me happy, stressed etc.)

good things that happened

things that sucked

self-care

overall mood today:

DAILY CHECK-IN, PLANNER, AND TRACKER

DATE: M T W T F S S Month: __________ Day: __________

today's intention

today's challenges

wake time: ______ a.m. bedtime: ______ p.m.

hours slept: ______

how rested i feel:

micro goals

priorities

optional

medication tracker	6am-10 am	10am-2pm	2pm-6pm	6pm-10pm	overnight
	additional:				

meal tracker

time	what i ate	how i felt

caffeine	
alcohol	
nicotine/vape	

physical activity

ostomy output tracker

bag changes										
bag empty/output	l s t	l s t	l s t	l s t	l s t	l s t	l s t	l s t	l s t	l s t
bag burp										

l = liquid output / s = semi-liquid/semi-thick / t = thick

symptom tracker

pain										
stress										
fatigue										
brain fog										
scale	1	2	3	4	5	6	7	8	9	10

pain triggers

depression / anxiety / stress / no meds/ poor sleep / lack of activity / weather / overdid it

pain type and location:

achy / burning / stabbing / cramping / shooting / heavy / sharp / weak / throbbing

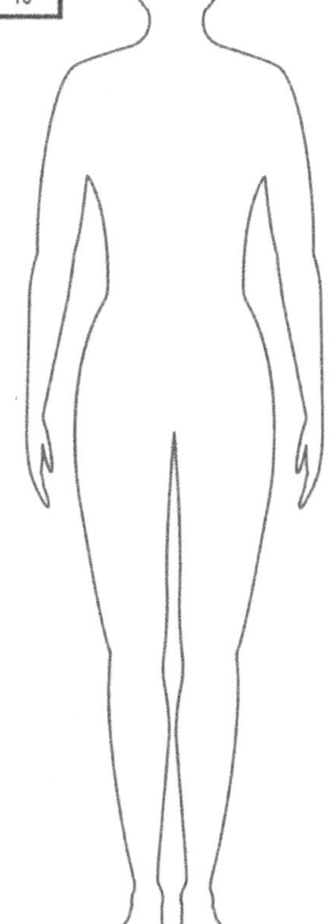

triggers
(what made me happy, stressed etc.)

good things that happened

things that sucked

self-care

overall mood today:

weekly review

week of: ____________________

my successes:

what i accepted:

what i let go:

what i did for self-care:

what was better this week:

what was worse this week:

pain summary:

medication/
care changes:

weekly planner

week of: ______________

what i will do for self-care:

what i'm looking forward to most:

what i have to get through:

how i will cope:

what i want to accomplish this week:

DAILY CHECK-IN, PLANNER, AND TRACKER

DATE: M T W T F S S Month: __________ Day: __________

today's intention

today's challenges

wake time: ______ a.m. bedtime: ______ p.m.

hours slept: ______

how rested i feel:

micro goals

priorities

optional

medication tracker	6am-10 am	10am-2pm	2pm-6pm	6pm-10pm	overnight
	additional:				

meal tracker

time	what i ate	how i felt

caffeine	
alcohol	
nicotine/vape	

physical activity

ostomy output tracker

bag changes										
bag empty/output	l s t	l s t	l s t	l s t	l s t	l s t	l s t	l s t	l s t	l s t
bag burp										

l = liquid output / s = semi-liquid/semi-thick / t = thick

symptom tracker

pain										
stress										
fatigue										
brain fog										
scale	1	2	3	4	5	6	7	8	9	10

pain triggers

depression / anxiety / stress / no meds/ poor sleep / lack of activity / weather / overdid it

pain type and location:

achy / burning / stabbing / cramping / shooting / heavy / sharp / weak / throbbing

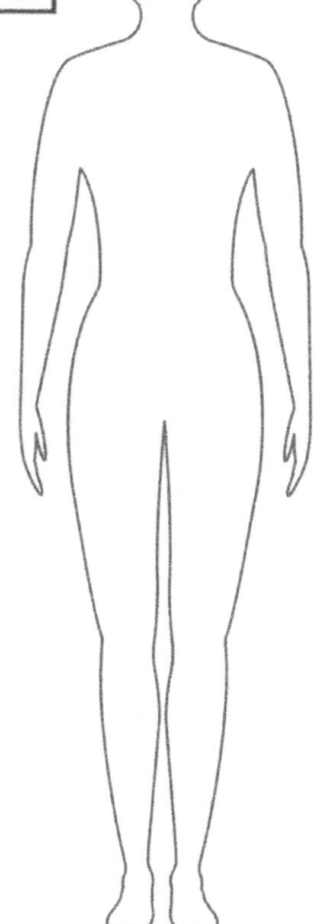

triggers (what made me happy, stressed etc.)	good things that happened	things that sucked

self-care

overall mood today:

DAILY CHECK-IN, PLANNER, AND TRACKER

DATE: M T W T F S S Month: __________ Day: __________

today's intention

today's challenges

wake time: ______ a.m. bedtime: ______ p.m.

hours slept: ______

how rested i feel:

micro goals

priorities

optional

medication tracker	6am-10 am	10am-2pm	2pm-6pm	6pm-10pm	overnight
	additional:				

meal tracker

time	what i ate	how i felt

caffeine	
alcohol	
nicotine/vape	

physical activity

ostomy output tracker

bag changes										
bag empty/output	l s t	l s t	l s t	l s t	l s t	l s t	l s t	l s t	l s t	l s t
bag burp										

l = liquid output / s = semi-liquid/semi-thick / t = thick

symptom tracker

pain										
stress										
fatigue										
brain fog										
scale	1	2	3	4	5	6	7	8	9	10

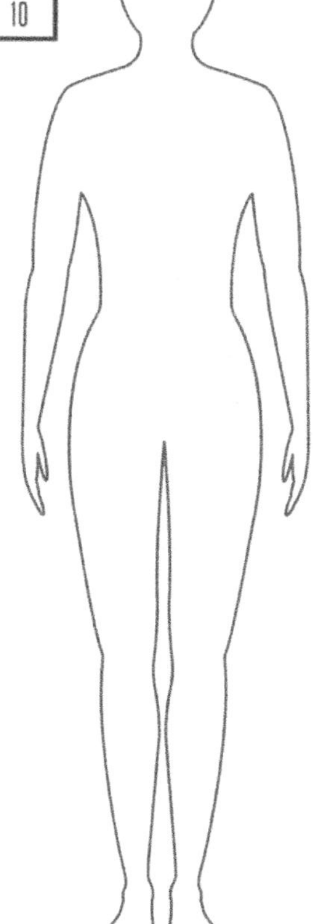

pain triggers

depression / anxiety / stress / no meds/ poor sleep / lack of activity / weather / overdid it

pain type and location:

achy / burning / stabbing / cramping / shooting / heavy / sharp / weak / throbbing

triggers
(what made me happy, stressed etc.)

good things that happened

things that sucked

self-care

overall mood today:

DAILY CHECK-IN, PLANNER, AND TRACKER

DATE: M T W T F S S Month: __________ Day: __________

today's intention

today's challenges

wake time: ______ a.m. bedtime: ______ p.m.

hours slept: ______

how rested i feel:

😄 😏 😕 ☹️ 😵

micro goals	priorities	optional

medication tracker	6am-10 am	10am-2pm	2pm-6pm	6pm-10pm	overnight
	additional:				

meal tracker

time	what i ate	how i felt

caffeine	
alcohol	
nicotine/vape	

physical activity

ostomy output tracker

bag changes										
bag empty/output	l s t	l s t	l s t	l s t	l s t	l s t	l s t	l s t	l s t	l s t
bag burp										

l = liquid output / s = semi-liquid/semi-thick / t = thick

symptom tracker

pain										
stress										
fatigue										
brain fog										
scale	1	2	3	4	5	6	7	8	9	10

pain triggers

depression / anxiety / stress / no meds/ poor sleep / lack of activity / weather / overdid it

pain type and location:

achy / burning / stabbing / cramping / shooting / heavy / sharp / weak / throbbing

triggers
(what made me happy, stressed etc.)

good things that happened

things that sucked

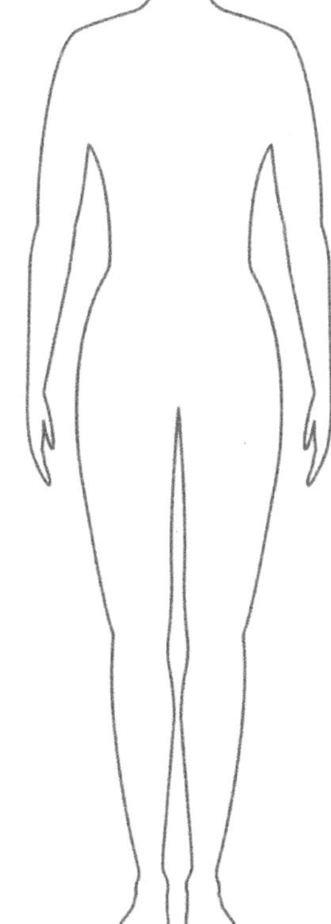

self-care

overall mood today:

DAILY CHECK-IN, PLANNER, AND TRACKER

DATE: M T W T F S S Month: __________ Day: __________

today's intention

today's challenges

wake time: ______ a.m. bedtime: ______ p.m.

hours slept: ______

how rested i feel:

micro goals

priorities

optional

medication tracker	6am-10 am	10am-2pm	2pm-6pm	6pm-10pm	overnight
	additional:				

meal tracker

time	what i ate	how i felt

caffeine	
alcohol	
nicotine/vape	

physical activity

ostomy output tracker

bag changes										
bag empty/output	l s t	l s t	l s t	l s t	l s t	l s t	l s t	l s t	l s t	l s t
bag burp										

l = liquid output / s = semi-liquid/semi-thick / t = thick

symptom tracker

pain										
stress										
fatigue										
brain fog										
scale	1	2	3	4	5	6	7	8	9	10

pain triggers

depression / anxiety / stress / no meds/ poor sleep / lack of activity / weather / overdid it

pain type and location:

achy / burning / stabbing / cramping / shooting / heavy / sharp / weak / throbbing

triggers
(what made me happy, stressed etc.)

good things that happened

things that sucked

self-care

overall mood today:

DAILY CHECK-IN, PLANNER, AND TRACKER

DATE: M T W T F S S Month: __________ Day: __________

today's intention

today's challenges

wake time: ______ a.m. bedtime: ______ p.m.

hours slept: ______

how rested i feel:

😄 🙂 😕 ☹️ 😵

micro goals	priorities	optional

medication tracker	6am-10 am	10am-2pm	2pm-6pm	6pm-10pm	overnight
	additional:				

meal tracker

time	what i ate	how i felt

caffeine	
alcohol	
nicotine/vape	

physical activity

ostomy output tracker

bag changes										
bag empty/output	l s t	l s t	l s t	l s t	l s t	l s t	l s t	l s t	l s t	l s t
bag burp										

l = liquid output / s = semi-liquid/semi-thick / t = thick

symptom tracker

pain										
stress										
fatigue										
brain fog										
scale	1	2	3	4	5	6	7	8	9	10

pain triggers

depression / anxiety / stress / no meds/ poor sleep / lack of activity / weather / overdid it

pain type and location:

achy / burning / stabbing / cramping / shooting / heavy / sharp / weak / throbbing

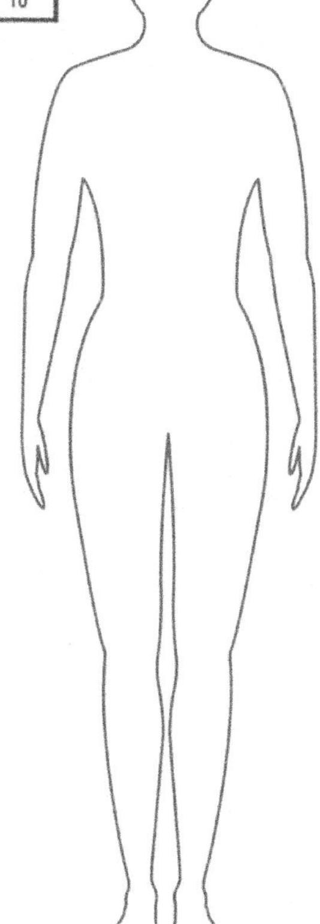

triggers
(what made me happy, stressed etc.)

good things that happened

things that sucked

self-care

overall mood today:

DAILY CHECK-IN, PLANNER, AND TRACKER

DATE: M T W T F S S Month: ________ Day: ________

today's intention

today's challenges

wake time: ______ a.m. bedtime: ______ p.m.

hours slept: ______

how rested i feel:

micro goals	priorities	optional

medication tracker	6am-10 am	10am-2pm	2pm-6pm	6pm-10pm	overnight
	additional:				

meal tracker

time	what i ate	how i felt

caffeine	
alcohol	
nicotine/vape	

physical activity

ostomy output tracker

bag changes										
bag empty/output	l s t	l s t	l s t	l s t	l s t	l s t	l s t	l s t	l s t	l s t
bag burp										

l = liquid output / s = semi-liquid/semi-thick / t = thick

symptom tracker

pain										
stress										
fatigue										
brain fog										
scale	1	2	3	4	5	6	7	8	9	10

pain triggers

depression / anxiety / stress / no meds/ poor sleep / lack of activity / weather / overdid it

pain type and location:

achy / burning / stabbing / cramping / shooting / heavy / sharp / weak / throbbing

triggers (what made me happy, stressed etc.)	good things that happened	things that sucked

self-care

DAILY CHECK-IN, PLANNER, AND TRACKER

DATE: M T W T F S S Month: ___________ Day: ___________

today's intention

today's challenges

wake time: _______ a.m. bedtime: _______ p.m.

hours slept: _______

how rested i feel:

micro goals	priorities	optional

medication tracker	6am-10 am	10am-2pm	2pm-6pm	6pm-10pm	overnight
	additional:				

meal tracker

time	what i ate	how i felt

caffeine	
alcohol	
nicotine/vape	

physical activity

ostomy output tracker

bag changes										
bag empty/output	l s t	l s t	l s t	l s t	l s t	l s t	l s t	l s t	l s t	l s t
bag burp										

l = liquid output / s = semi-liquid/semi-thick / t = thick

symptom tracker

pain										
stress										
fatigue										
brain fog										
scale	1	2	3	4	5	6	7	8	9	10

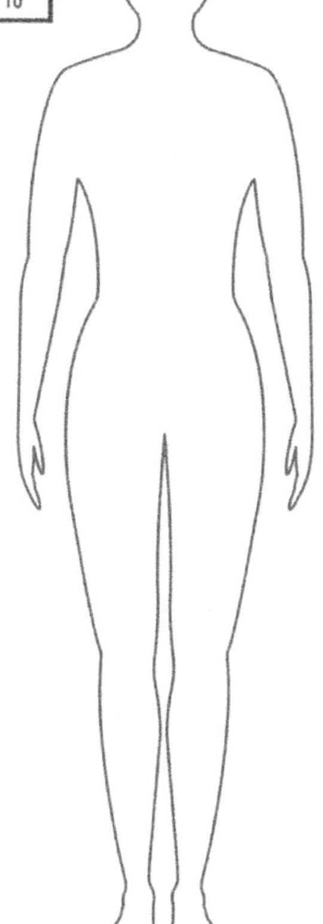

pain triggers

depression / anxiety / stress / no meds/ poor sleep / lack of activity / weather / overdid it

pain type and location:

achy / burning / stabbing / cramping / shooting / heavy / sharp / weak / throbbing

triggers
(what made me happy, stressed etc.)

good things that happened

things that sucked

self-care

overall mood today:

weekly review

week of: ____________________

my successes:

what i accepted:

what i let go:

what i did for self-care:

what was better this week:

what was worse this week:

pain summary:

medication/
care changes:

weekly planner

week of: ______________

what i will do for self-care:

what i'm looking forward to most:

what i have to get through:

how i will cope:

what i want to accomplish this week:

DAILY CHECK-IN, PLANNER, AND TRACKER

DATE: M T W T F S S Month: __________ Day: __________

today's intention

today's challenges

wake time: ______ a.m. bedtime: ______ p.m.

hours slept: ______

how rested i feel:

micro goals

priorities

optional

medication tracker	6am-10 am	10am-2pm	2pm-6pm	6pm-10pm	overnight
	additional:				

meal tracker

time	what i ate	how i felt

caffeine	
alcohol	
nicotine/vape	

physical activity

ostomy output tracker

bag changes										
bag empty/output	l s t	l s t	l s t	l s t	l s t	l s t	l s t	l s t	l s t	l s t
bag burp										

l = liquid output / s = semi-liquid/semi-thick / t = thick

symptom tracker

pain										
stress										
fatigue										
brain fog										
scale	1	2	3	4	5	6	7	8	9	10

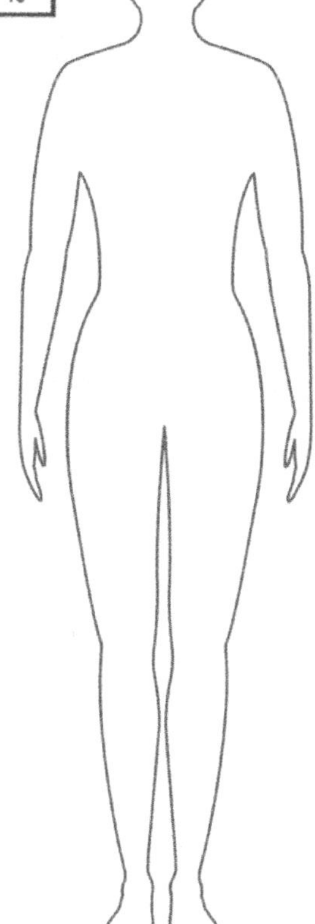

pain triggers

depression / anxiety / stress / no meds/ poor sleep / lack of activity / weather / overdid it

pain type and location:

achy / burning / stabbing / cramping / shooting / heavy / sharp / weak / throbbing

triggers
(what made me happy, stressed etc.)

good things that happened

things that sucked

self-care

overall mood today:

DAILY CHECK-IN, PLANNER, AND TRACKER

DATE: M T W T F S S Month: __________ Day: __________

today's intention

today's challenges

wake time: ______ a.m. bedtime: ______ p.m.

hours slept: ______

how rested i feel:

micro goals

priorities

optional

medication tracker	6am-10 am	10am-2pm	2pm-6pm	6pm-10pm	overnight
	additional:				

meal tracker

time	what i ate	how i felt

caffeine	
alcohol	
nicotine/vape	

physical activity

ostomy output tracker

bag changes										
bag empty/output	l s t	l s t	l s t	l s t	l s t	l s t	l s t	l s t	l s t	l s t
bag burp										

l = liquid output / s = semi-liquid/semi-thick / t = thick

symptom tracker

pain										
stress										
fatigue										
brain fog										
scale	1	2	3	4	5	6	7	8	9	10

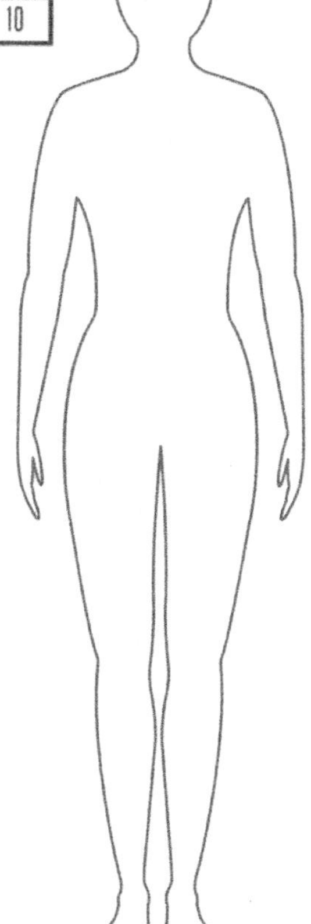

pain triggers

depression / anxiety / stress / no meds/ poor sleep / lack of activity / weather / overdid it

pain type and location:

achy / burning / stabbing / cramping / shooting / heavy / sharp / weak / throbbing

triggers
(what made me happy, stressed etc.)

good things that happened

things that sucked

self-care

overall mood today:

DAILY CHECK-IN, PLANNER, AND TRACKER

DATE: M T W T F S S Month: ___________ Day: ___________

today's intention

today's challenges

wake time: _______ a.m. bedtime: _______ p.m.

hours slept: _______

how rested i feel:

micro goals

priorities

optional

medication tracker	6am-10 am	10am-2pm	2pm-6pm	6pm-10pm	overnight
	additional:				

meal tracker

time	what i ate	how i felt

caffeine	
alcohol	
nicotine/vape	

physical activity

ostomy output tracker

bag changes										
bag empty/output	l s t	l s t	l s t	l s t	l s t	l s t	l s t	l s t	l s t	l s t
bag burp										

l = liquid output / s = semi-liquid/semi-thick / t = thick

symptom tracker

pain										
stress										
fatigue										
brain fog										
scale	1	2	3	4	5	6	7	8	9	10

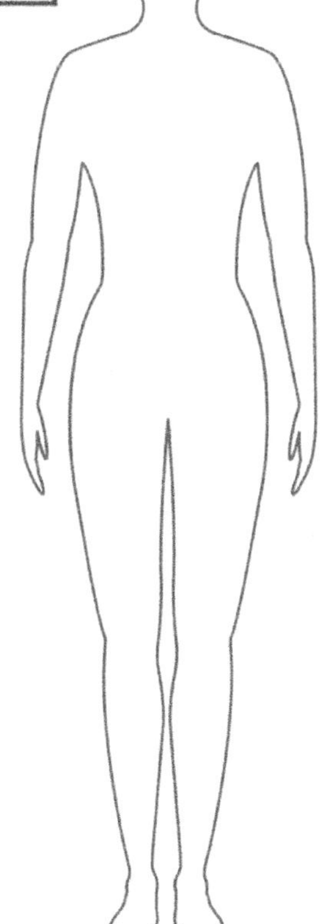

pain triggers

depression / anxiety / stress / no meds/ poor sleep / lack of activity / weather / overdid it

pain type and location:

achy / burning / stabbing / cramping / shooting / heavy / sharp / weak / throbbing

triggers
(what made me happy, stressed etc.)

good things that happened

things that sucked

self-care

overall mood today:

DAILY CHECK-IN, PLANNER, AND TRACKER

DATE: M T W T F S S Month: __________ Day: __________

today's intention

today's challenges

wake time: ______ a.m. bedtime: ______ p.m.

hours slept: ______

how rested i feel:

😄 🙂 😕 ☹️ 😵

micro goals	priorities	optional

medication tracker	6am-10 am	10am-2pm	2pm-6pm	6pm-10pm	overnight
	additional:				

meal tracker

time	what i ate	how i felt

caffeine	
alcohol	
nicotine/vape	

physical activity

ostomy output tracker

bag changes										
bag empty/output	l s t	l s t	l s t	l s t	l s t	l s t	l s t	l s t	l s t	l s t
bag burp										

l = liquid output / s = semi-liquid/semi-thick / t = thick

symptom tracker

pain										
stress										
fatigue										
brain fog										
scale	1	2	3	4	5	6	7	8	9	10

pain triggers

depression / anxiety / stress / no meds/ poor sleep / lack of activity / weather / overdid it

pain type and location:

achy / burning / stabbing / cramping / shooting / heavy / sharp / weak / throbbing

triggers (what made me happy, stressed etc.)	good things that happened	things that sucked

self-care

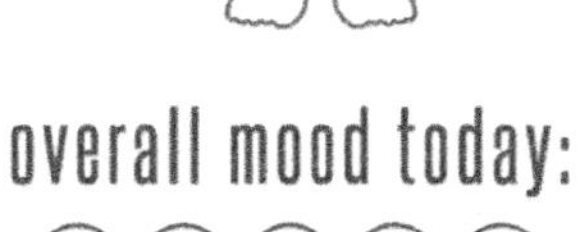

overall mood today:

DAILY CHECK-IN, PLANNER, AND TRACKER

DATE: M T W T F S S Month: __________ Day: __________

today's intention

today's challenges

wake time: ______ a.m. bedtime: ______ p.m.

hours slept: ______

how rested i feel:

micro goals

priorities

optional

medication tracker	6am-10 am	10am-2pm	2pm-6pm	6pm-10pm	overnight
	additional:				

meal tracker

time	what i ate	how i felt

caffeine	
alcohol	
nicotine/vape	

physical activity

ostomy output tracker

bag changes										
bag empty/output	l s t	l s t	l s t	l s t	l s t	l s t	l s t	l s t	l s t	l s t
bag burp										

l = liquid output / s = semi-liquid/semi-thick / t = thick

symptom tracker

pain										
stress										
fatigue										
brain fog										
scale	1	2	3	4	5	6	7	8	9	10

pain triggers

depression / anxiety / stress / no meds/ poor sleep / lack of activity / weather / overdid it

pain type and location:

achy / burning / stabbing / cramping / shooting / heavy / sharp / weak / throbbing

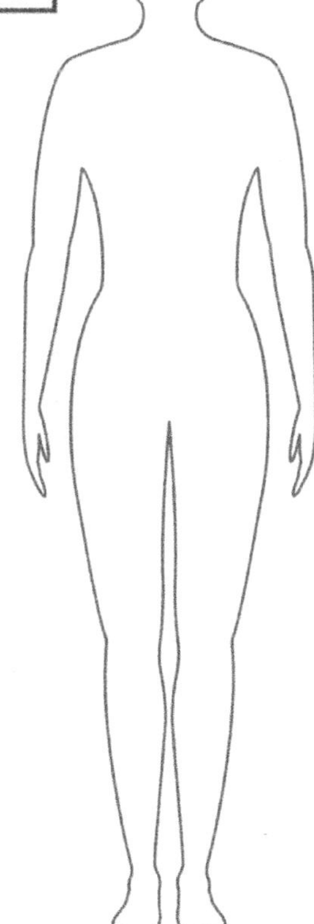

triggers
(what made me happy, stressed etc.)

good things that happened

things that sucked

self-care

overall mood today:

DAILY CHECK-IN, PLANNER, AND TRACKER

DATE: M T W T F S S Month: ___________ Day: ___________

today's intention

today's challenges

wake time: ______ a.m. bedtime: ______ p.m.

hours slept: ______

how rested i feel:

micro goals

priorities

optional

medication tracker	6am-10 am	10am-2pm	2pm-6pm	6pm-10pm	overnight
	additional:				

meal tracker

time	what i ate	how i felt

caffeine	
alcohol	
nicotine/vape	

physical activity

ostomy output tracker

bag changes										
bag empty/output	l s t	l s t	l s t	l s t	l s t	l s t	l s t	l s t	l s t	l s t
bag burp										

l = liquid output / s = semi-liquid/semi-thick / t = thick

symptom tracker

pain										
stress										
fatigue										
brain fog										
scale	1	2	3	4	5	6	7	8	9	10

pain triggers

depression / anxiety / stress / no meds/ poor sleep / lack of activity / weather / overdid it

pain type and location:

achy / burning / stabbing / cramping / shooting / heavy / sharp / weak / throbbing

triggers
(what made me happy, stressed etc.)

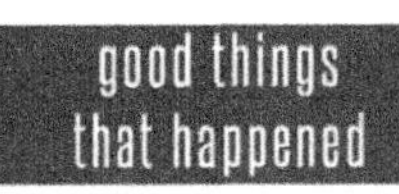

good things that happened

things that sucked

self-care

overall mood today:

DAILY CHECK-IN, PLANNER, AND TRACKER

DATE: M T W T F S S Month: __________ Day: __________

today's intention

today's challenges

wake time: ______ a.m. bedtime: ______ p.m.

hours slept: ______

how rested i feel:

micro goals	priorities	optional

medication tracker	6am-10 am	10am-2pm	2pm-6pm	6pm-10pm	overnight
	additional:				

meal tracker

time	what i ate	how i felt

caffeine	
alcohol	
nicotine/vape	

physical activity

ostomy output tracker

bag changes										
bag empty/output	l s t	l s t	l s t	l s t	l s t	l s t	l s t	l s t	l s t	l s t
bag burp										

l = liquid output / s = semi-liquid/semi-thick / t = thick

symptom tracker

pain										
stress										
fatigue										
brain fog										
scale	1	2	3	4	5	6	7	8	9	10

pain triggers

depression / anxiety / stress / no meds/ poor sleep / lack of activity / weather / overdid it

pain type and location:

achy / burning / stabbing / cramping / shooting / heavy / sharp / weak / throbbing

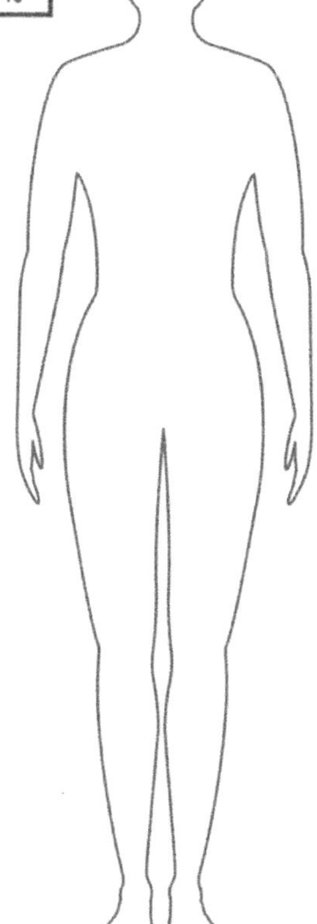

triggers
(what made me happy, stressed etc.)

good things that happened

things that sucked

self-care

overall mood today:

weekly review

week of: ____________________

my successes:

what i accepted:

what i let go:

what i did for self-care:

what was better this week:

what was worse this week:

pain summary:

medication/ care changes:

weekly planner

week of: ______________

what i will do for self-care:

what i'm looking forward to most:

what i have to get through:

how i will cope:

what i want to accomplish this week:

DAILY CHECK-IN, PLANNER, AND TRACKER

DATE: M T W T F S S Month: ___________ Day: ___________

today's intention

today's challenges

wake time: _______ a.m. bedtime: _______ p.m.

hours slept: _______

how rested i feel:

😄 🙂 😕 ☹️ 😵

micro goals	priorities	optional

medication tracker	6am-10 am	10am-2pm	2pm-6pm	6pm-10pm	overnight
	additional:				

meal tracker

time	what i ate	how i felt

caffeine	
alcohol	
nicotine/vape	

physical activity

ostomy output tracker

bag changes										
bag empty/output	l s t	l s t	l s t	l s t	l s t	l s t	l s t	l s t	l s t	l s t
bag burp										

l = liquid output / s = semi-liquid/semi-thick / t = thick

symptom tracker

pain										
stress										
fatigue										
brain fog										
scale	1	2	3	4	5	6	7	8	9	10

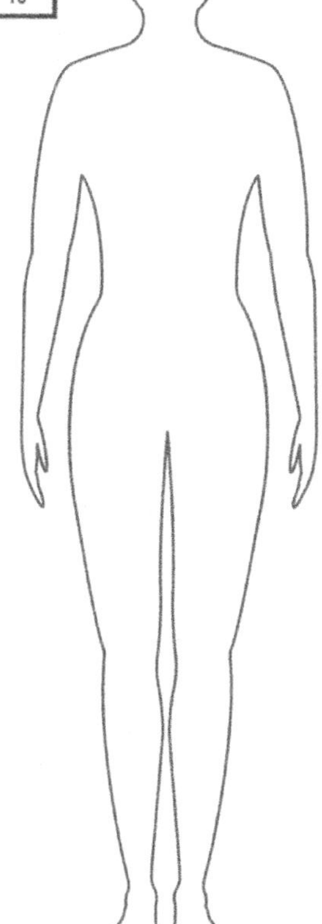

pain triggers

depression / anxiety / stress / no meds/ poor sleep / lack of activity / weather / overdid it

pain type and location:

achy / burning / stabbing / cramping / shooting / heavy / sharp / weak / throbbing

triggers
(what made me happy, stressed etc.)

good things that happened

things that sucked

self-care

overall mood today:

DAILY CHECK-IN, PLANNER, AND TRACKER

DATE: M T W T F S S Month: ___________ Day: ___________

today's intention

today's challenges

wake time: ______ a.m. bedtime: ______ p.m.

hours slept: ______

how rested i feel:

micro goals

priorities

optional

medication tracker	6am-10 am	10am-2pm	2pm-6pm	6pm-10pm	overnight
	additional:				

meal tracker

time	what i ate	how i felt

caffeine	
alcohol	
nicotine/vape	

physical activity

ostomy output tracker

bag changes										
bag empty/output	l s t	l s t	l s t	l s t	l s t	l s t	l s t	l s t	l s t	l s t
bag burp										

l = liquid output / s = semi-liquid/semi-thick / t = thick

symptom tracker

pain										
stress										
fatigue										
brain fog										
scale	1	2	3	4	5	6	7	8	9	10

pain triggers

depression / anxiety / stress / no meds/ poor sleep / lack of activity / weather / overdid it

pain type and location:

achy / burning / stabbing / cramping / shooting / heavy / sharp / weak / throbbing

triggers
(what made me happy, stressed etc.)

good things that happened

things that sucked

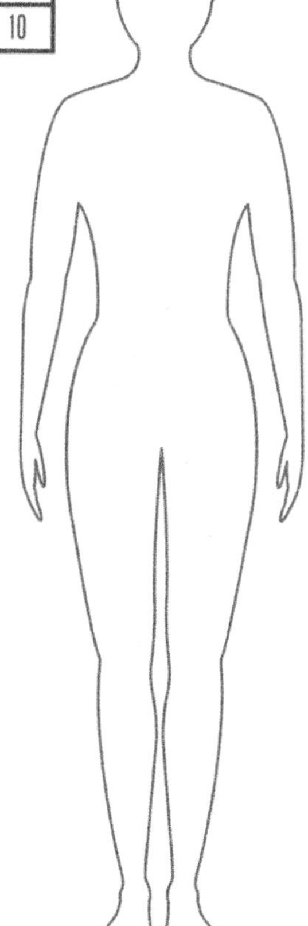

self-care

overall mood today:

DAILY CHECK-IN, PLANNER, AND TRACKER

DATE: M T W T F S S Month: ____________ Day: ____________

today's intention

today's challenges

wake time: _______ a.m. bedtime: _______ p.m.

hours slept: _______

how rested i feel:

micro goals

priorities

optional

medication tracker	6am-10 am	10am-2pm	2pm-6pm	6pm-10pm	overnight
	additional:				

meal tracker

time	what i ate	how i felt

caffeine	
alcohol	
nicotine/vape	

physical activity

ostomy output tracker

bag changes										
bag empty/output	l s t	l s t	l s t	l s t	l s t	l s t	l s t	l s t	l s t	l s t
bag burp										

l = liquid output / s = semi-liquid/semi-thick / t = thick

symptom tracker

pain										
stress										
fatigue										
brain fog										
scale	1	2	3	4	5	6	7	8	9	10

pain triggers

depression / anxiety / stress / no meds/ poor sleep / lack of activity / weather / overdid it

pain type and location:

achy / burning / stabbing / cramping / shooting / heavy / sharp / weak / throbbing

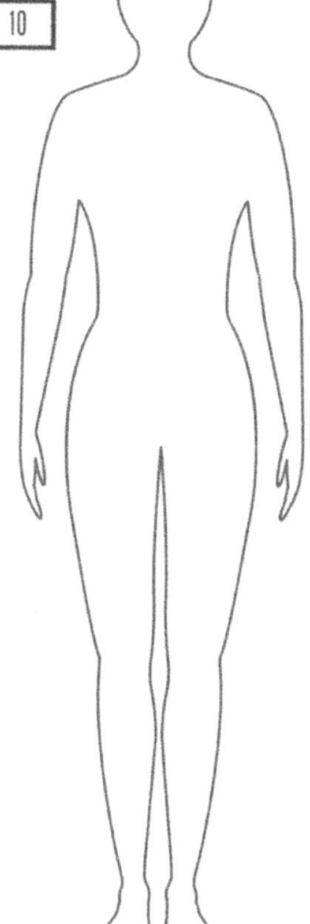

triggers (what made me happy, stressed etc.)	good things that happened	things that sucked

self-care

overall mood today:

weekly review

week of: ____________________

my successes:

what i accepted:

what i let go:

what i did for self-care:

what was better this week:

what was worse this week:

pain summary:

medication/
care changes:

monthly review

month: ______________

my successes:

what i accepted:

what i let go:

what i did for self-care:

what was better this month:

what was worse this month:

pain summary:

medication/
care changes:

notes:

monthly planner

month: ____________

what i will do for self-care:

what i'm looking forward to most:

what i have to get through:

how i will cope:

what i want to accomplish this month:

appointment tracker

date	time	doctor	location	issue	outcome

current medications

name	dose	times per day/week/month	side effects	refill on:

new treatment/medication:

weekly planner

week of: ______________

what i will do for self-care:

what i'm looking forward to most:

what i have to get through:

how i will cope:

what i want to accomplish this week:

DAILY CHECK-IN, PLANNER, AND TRACKER

DATE: M T W T F S S Month: __________ Day: __________

today's intention

today's challenges

wake time: _______ a.m. bedtime: _______ p.m.

hours slept: _______

how rested i feel:

micro goals

priorities

optional

medication tracker	6am-10 am	10am-2pm	2pm-6pm	6pm-10pm	overnight
	additional:				

meal tracker

time	what i ate	how i felt

caffeine	
alcohol	
nicotine/vape	

physical activity

ostomy output tracker

bag changes										
bag empty/output	l s t	l s t	l s t	l s t	l s t	l s t	l s t	l s t	l s t	l s t
bag burp										

l = liquid output / s = semi-liquid/semi-thick / t = thick

symptom tracker

pain										
stress										
fatigue										
brain fog										
scale	1	2	3	4	5	6	7	8	9	10

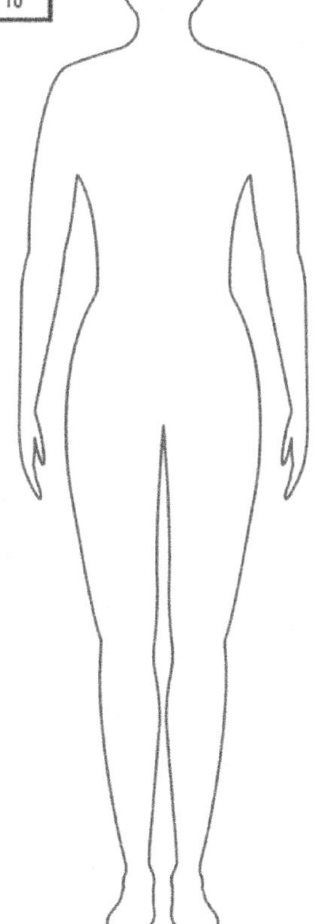

pain triggers

depression / anxiety / stress / no meds/ poor sleep / lack of activity / weather / overdid it

pain type and location:

achy / burning / stabbing / cramping / shooting / heavy / sharp / weak / throbbing

triggers (what made me happy, stressed etc.)	good things that happened	things that sucked

self-care

overall mood today:

DAILY CHECK-IN, PLANNER, AND TRACKER

DATE: M T W T F S S Month: __________ Day: __________

today's intention

today's challenges

wake time: ______ a.m. bedtime: ______ p.m.

hours slept: ______

how rested i feel:

micro goals

priorities

optional

medication tracker	6am-10 am	10am-2pm	2pm-6pm	6pm-10pm	overnight
	additional:				

meal tracker

time	what i ate	how i felt

caffeine	
alcohol	
nicotine/vape	

physical activity

ostomy output tracker

bag changes										
bag empty/output	l s t	l s t	l s t	l s t	l s t	l s t	l s t	l s t	l s t	l s t
bag burp										

l = liquid output / s = semi-liquid/semi-thick / t = thick

symptom tracker

pain										
stress										
fatigue										
brain fog										
scale	1	2	3	4	5	6	7	8	9	10

pain triggers

depression / anxiety / stress / no meds/ poor sleep / lack of activity / weather / overdid it

pain type and location:

achy / burning / stabbing / cramping / shooting / heavy / sharp / weak / throbbing

triggers
(what made me happy, stressed etc.)

good things that happened

things that sucked

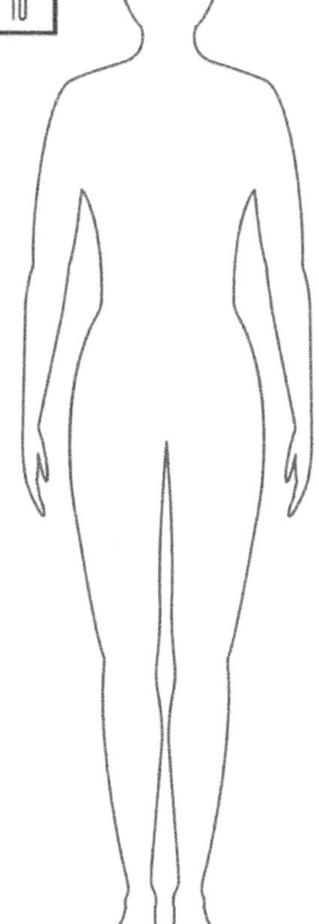

self-care

overall mood today:

DAILY CHECK-IN, PLANNER, AND TRACKER

DATE: M T W T F S S Month: __________ Day: __________

today's intention

today's challenges

wake time: ______ a.m. bedtime: ______ p.m.

hours slept: ______

how rested i feel:

😄 😏 😕 ☹️ 😵

micro goals	priorities	optional

medication tracker	6am-10 am	10am-2pm	2pm-6pm	6pm-10pm	overnight
	additional:				

meal tracker

time	what i ate	how i felt

caffeine	
alcohol	
nicotine/vape	

physical activity

ostomy output tracker

bag changes										
bag empty/output	l s t	l s t	l s t	l s t	l s t	l s t	l s t	l s t	l s t	l s t
bag burp										

l = liquid output / s = semi-liquid/semi-thick / t = thick

symptom tracker

pain										
stress										
fatigue										
brain fog										
scale	1	2	3	4	5	6	7	8	9	10

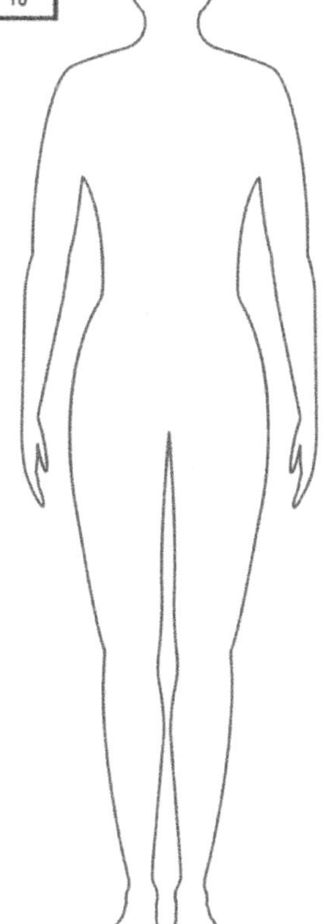

pain triggers

depression / anxiety / stress / no meds/ poor sleep / lack of activity / weather / overdid it

pain type and location:

achy / burning / stabbing / cramping / shooting / heavy / sharp / weak / throbbing

triggers
(what made me happy, stressed etc.)

good things that happened

things that sucked

self-care

overall mood today:

DAILY CHECK-IN, PLANNER, AND TRACKER

DATE: M T W T F S S Month: __________ Day: __________

today's intention

today's challenges

wake time: ______ a.m. bedtime: ______ p.m.

hours slept: ______

how rested i feel:

micro goals

priorities

optional

medication tracker	6am-10 am	10am-2pm	2pm-6pm	6pm-10pm	overnight
	additional:				

meal tracker

time	what i ate	how i felt

caffeine	
alcohol	
nicotine/vape	

physical activity

ostomy output tracker

bag changes										
bag empty/output	l s t	l s t	l s t	l s t	l s t	l s t	l s t	l s t	l s t	l s t
bag burp										

l = liquid output / s = semi-liquid/semi-thick / t = thick

symptom tracker

pain										
stress										
fatigue										
brain fog										
scale	1	2	3	4	5	6	7	8	9	10

pain triggers

depression / anxiety / stress / no meds/ poor sleep / lack of activity / weather / overdid it

pain type and location:

achy / burning / stabbing / cramping / shooting / heavy / sharp / weak / throbbing

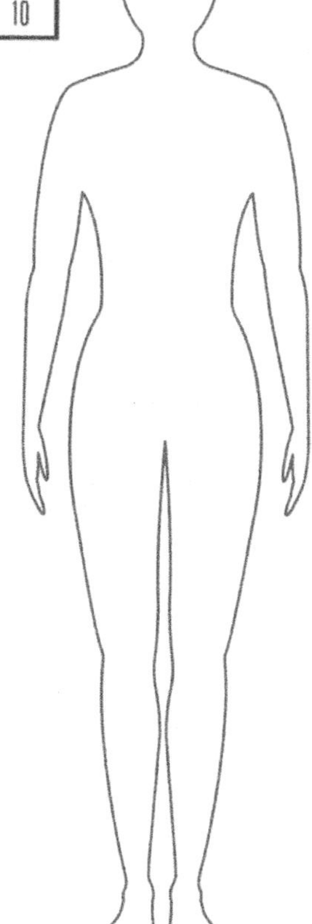

triggers
(what made me happy, stressed etc.)

good things that happened

things that sucked

self-care

overall mood today:

DAILY CHECK-IN, PLANNER, AND TRACKER

DATE: M T W T F S S Month: __________ Day: __________

today's intention

today's challenges

wake time: ______ a.m. bedtime: ______ p.m.

hours slept: ______

how rested i feel:

micro goals

priorities

optional

medication tracker	6am-10 am	10am-2pm	2pm-6pm	6pm-10pm	overnight
	additional:				

meal tracker

time	what i ate	how i felt

caffeine	
alcohol	
nicotine/vape	

physical activity

ostomy output tracker

bag changes										
bag empty/output	l s t	l s t	l s t	l s t	l s t	l s t	l s t	l s t	l s t	l s t
bag burp										

l = liquid output / s = semi-liquid/semi-thick / t = thick

symptom tracker

pain										
stress										
fatigue										
brain fog										
scale	1	2	3	4	5	6	7	8	9	10

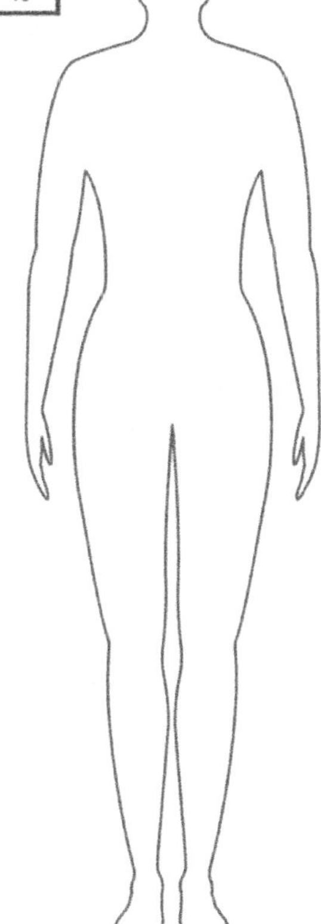

pain triggers

depression / anxiety / stress / no meds/ poor sleep / lack of activity / weather / overdid it

pain type and location:

achy / burning / stabbing / cramping / shooting / heavy / sharp / weak / throbbing

triggers
(what made me happy, stressed etc.)

good things that happened

things that sucked

self-care

overall mood today:

DAILY CHECK-IN, PLANNER, AND TRACKER

DATE: M T W T F S S Month: ___________ Day: ___________

today's intention

today's challenges

wake time: ______ a.m. bedtime: ______ p.m.

hours slept: ______

how rested i feel:

micro goals

priorities

optional

medication tracker	6am-10 am	10am-2pm	2pm-6pm	6pm-10pm	overnight
	additional:				

meal tracker

time	what i ate	how i felt

caffeine	
alcohol	
nicotine/vape	

physical activity

ostomy output tracker

bag changes										
bag empty/output	l s t	l s t	l s t	l s t	l s t	l s t	l s t	l s t	l s t	l s t
bag burp										

l = liquid output / s = semi-liquid/semi-thick / t = thick

symptom tracker

pain										
stress										
fatigue										
brain fog										
scale	1	2	3	4	5	6	7	8	9	10

pain triggers

depression / anxiety / stress / no meds/ poor sleep / lack of activity / weather / overdid it

pain type and location:

achy / burning / stabbing / cramping / shooting / heavy / sharp / weak / throbbing

triggers
(what made me happy, stressed etc.)

good things that happened

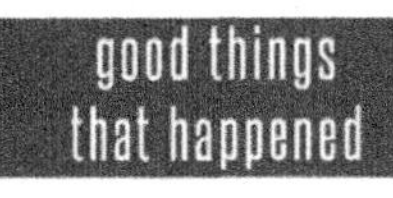

things that sucked

self-care

overall mood today:

DAILY CHECK-IN, PLANNER, AND TRACKER

DATE: M T W T F S S Month: ___________ Day: ___________

today's intention

today's challenges

wake time: _______ a.m. bedtime: _______ p.m.

hours slept: _______

how rested i feel:

micro goals	priorities	optional

medication tracker	6am-10 am	10am-2pm	2pm-6pm	6pm-10pm	overnight
	additional:				

meal tracker

time	what i ate	how i felt

caffeine	
alcohol	
nicotine/vape	

physical activity

ostomy output tracker

bag changes										
bag empty/output	l s t	l s t	l s t	l s t	l s t	l s t	l s t	l s t	l s t	l s t
bag burp										

l = liquid output / s = semi-liquid/semi-thick / t = thick

symptom tracker

pain										
stress										
fatigue										
brain fog										
scale	1	2	3	4	5	6	7	8	9	10

pain triggers

depression / anxiety / stress / no meds/ poor sleep / lack of activity / weather / overdid it

pain type and location:

achy / burning / stabbing / cramping / shooting / heavy / sharp / weak / throbbing

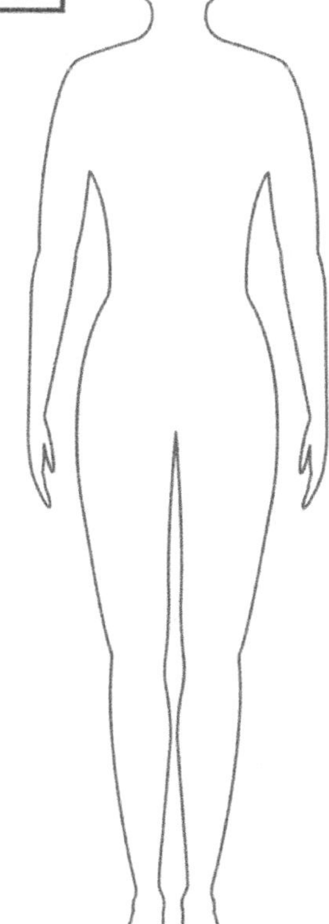

triggers
(what made me happy, stressed etc.)

good things that happened

things that sucked

self-care

overall mood today:

weekly review

week of: ____________________

my successes:

what i accepted:

what i let go:

what i did for self-care:

what was better this week:

what was worse this week:

pain summary:

medication/
care changes:

weekly planner

week of: ___________

what i will do for self-care:

what i'm looking forward to most:

what i have to get through:

how i will cope:

what i want to accomplish this week:

DAILY CHECK-IN, PLANNER, AND TRACKER

DATE: M T W T F S S Month: __________ Day: __________

today's intention

today's challenges

wake time: ______ a.m. bedtime: ______ p.m.

hours slept: ______

how rested i feel:

micro goals

priorities

optional

medication tracker	6am-10 am	10am-2pm	2pm-6pm	6pm-10pm	overnight
	additional:				

meal tracker

time	what i ate	how i felt

caffeine	
alcohol	
nicotine/vape	

physical activity

ostomy output tracker

bag changes										
bag empty/output	l s t	l s t	l s t	l s t	l s t	l s t	l s t	l s t	l s t	l s t
bag burp										

l = liquid output / s = semi-liquid/semi-thick / t = thick

symptom tracker

pain										
stress										
fatigue										
brain fog										
scale	1	2	3	4	5	6	7	8	9	10

pain triggers

depression / anxiety / stress / no meds/ poor sleep / lack of activity / weather / overdid it

pain type and location:

achy / burning / stabbing / cramping / shooting / heavy / sharp / weak / throbbing

triggers
(what made me happy, stressed etc.)

good things that happened

things that sucked

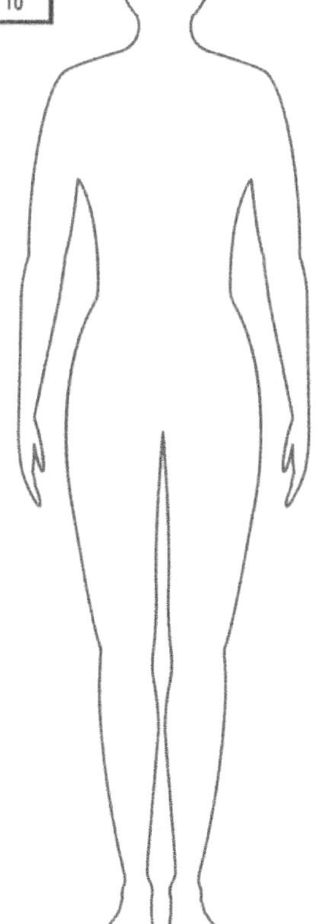

self-care

overall mood today:

DAILY CHECK-IN, PLANNER, AND TRACKER

DATE: M T W T F S S Month: __________ Day: __________

today's intention

today's challenges

wake time: ______ a.m. bedtime: ______ p.m.

hours slept: ______

how rested i feel:

micro goals

priorities

optional

medication tracker	6am-10 am	10am-2pm	2pm-6pm	6pm-10pm	overnight
	additional:				

meal tracker

time	what i ate	how i felt

caffeine	
alcohol	
nicotine/vape	

physical activity

ostomy output tracker

bag changes										
bag empty/output	l s t	l s t	l s t	l s t	l s t	l s t	l s t	l s t	l s t	l s t
bag burp										

l = liquid output / s = semi-liquid/semi-thick / t = thick

symptom tracker

pain										
stress										
fatigue										
brain fog										
scale	1	2	3	4	5	6	7	8	9	10

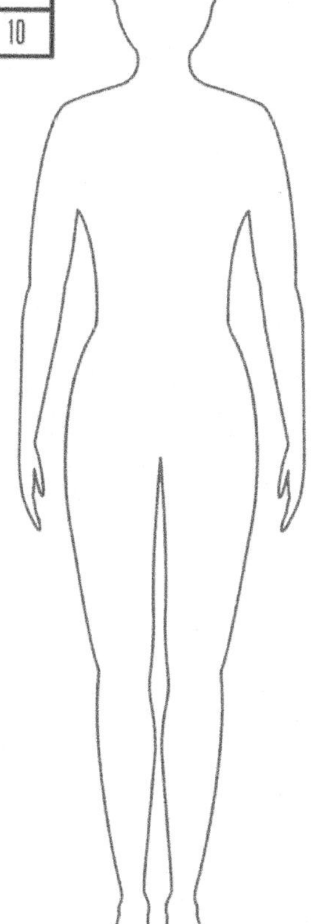

pain triggers

depression / anxiety / stress / no meds/ poor sleep / lack of activity / weather / overdid it

pain type and location:

achy / burning / stabbing / cramping / shooting / heavy / sharp / weak / throbbing

triggers
(what made me happy, stressed etc.)

good things that happened

things that sucked

self-care

overall mood today:

DAILY CHECK-IN, PLANNER, AND TRACKER

DATE: M T W T F S S Month: __________ Day: __________

today's intention

today's challenges

wake time: ______ a.m. bedtime: ______ p.m.

hours slept: ______

how rested i feel:

micro goals	priorities	optional

medication tracker	6am-10 am	10am-2pm	2pm-6pm	6pm-10pm	overnight
	additional:				

meal tracker

time	what i ate	how i felt

caffeine	
alcohol	
nicotine/vape	

physical activity

ostomy output tracker

bag changes										
bag empty/output	l s t	l s t	l s t	l s t	l s t	l s t	l s t	l s t	l s t	l s t
bag burp										

l = liquid output / s = semi-liquid/semi-thick / t = thick

symptom tracker

pain										
stress										
fatigue										
brain fog										
scale	1	2	3	4	5	6	7	8	9	10

pain triggers

depression / anxiety / stress / no meds/ poor sleep / lack of activity / weather / overdid it

pain type and location:

achy / burning / stabbing / cramping / shooting / heavy / sharp / weak / throbbing

triggers
(what made me happy, stressed etc.)

good things that happened

things that sucked

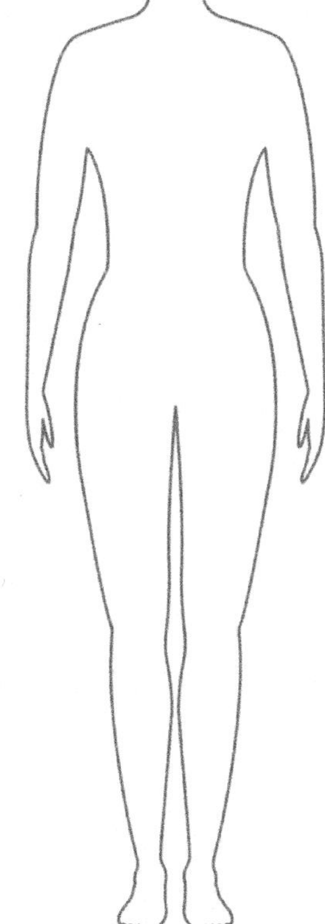

self-care

overall mood today:

DAILY CHECK-IN, PLANNER, AND TRACKER

DATE: M T W T F S S Month: ___________ Day: ___________

today's intention

today's challenges

wake time: _______ a.m. bedtime: _______ p.m.

hours slept: _______

how rested i feel:

micro goals	priorities	optional

medication tracker	6am-10 am	10am-2pm	2pm-6pm	6pm-10pm	overnight
	additional:				

meal tracker

time	what i ate	how i felt

caffeine	
alcohol	
nicotine/vape	

physical activity

ostomy output tracker

bag changes										
bag empty/output	l s t	l s t	l s t	l s t	l s t	l s t	l s t	l s t	l s t	l s t
bag burp										

l = liquid output / s = semi-liquid/semi-thick / t = thick

symptom tracker

pain										
stress										
fatigue										
brain fog										
scale	1	2	3	4	5	6	7	8	9	10

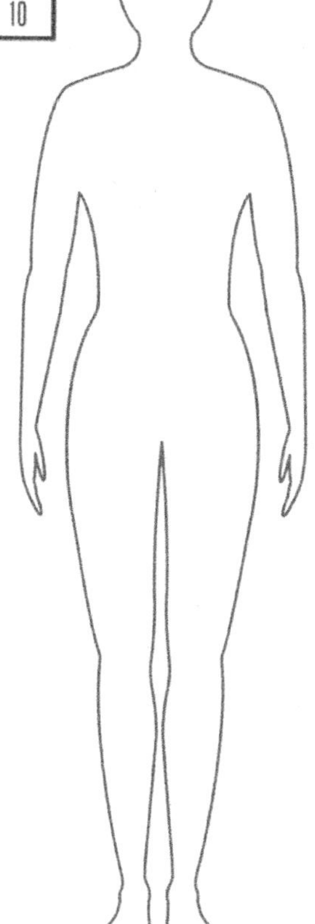

pain triggers

depression / anxiety / stress / no meds/ poor sleep / lack of activity / weather / overdid it

pain type and location:

achy / burning / stabbing / cramping / shooting / heavy / sharp / weak / throbbing

triggers
(what made me happy, stressed etc.)

good things that happened

things that sucked

self-care

overall mood today:

DAILY CHECK-IN, PLANNER, AND TRACKER

DATE: M T W T F S S Month: __________ Day: __________

today's intention

today's challenges

wake time: ______ a.m. bedtime: ______ p.m.

hours slept: ______

how rested i feel:

micro goals

priorities

optional

medication tracker	6am-10 am	10am-2pm	2pm-6pm	6pm-10pm	overnight
	additional:				

meal tracker

time	what i ate	how i felt

caffeine	
alcohol	
nicotine/vape	

physical activity

ostomy output tracker

bag changes										
bag empty/output	l s t	l s t	l s t	l s t	l s t	l s t	l s t	l s t	l s t	l s t
bag burp										

l = liquid output / s = semi-liquid/semi-thick / t = thick

symptom tracker

pain										
stress										
fatigue										
brain fog										
scale	1	2	3	4	5	6	7	8	9	10

pain triggers

depression / anxiety / stress / no meds/ poor sleep / lack of activity / weather / overdid it

pain type and location:

achy / burning / stabbing / cramping / shooting / heavy / sharp / weak / throbbing

triggers
(what made me happy, stressed etc.)

good things that happened

things that sucked

self-care

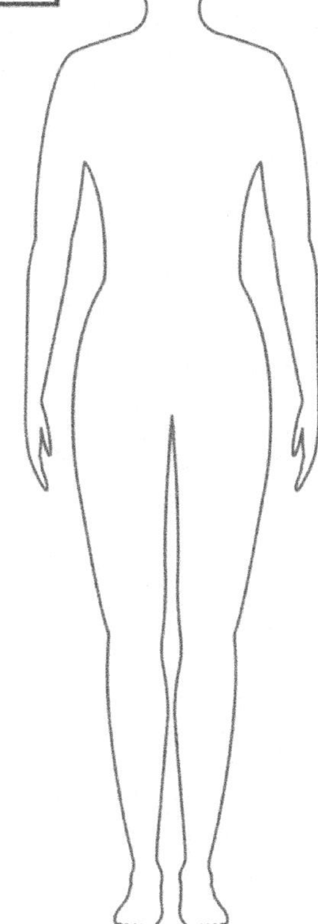

overall mood today:

DAILY CHECK-IN, PLANNER, AND TRACKER

DATE: M T W T F S S Month: __________ Day: __________

today's intention

today's challenges

wake time: ______ a.m. bedtime: ______ p.m.

hours slept: ______

how rested i feel:

micro goals

priorities

optional

medication tracker	6am-10 am	10am-2pm	2pm-6pm	6pm-10pm	overnight
	additional:				

meal tracker

time	what i ate	how i felt

caffeine	
alcohol	
nicotine/vape	

physical activity

ostomy output tracker

bag changes										
bag empty/output	l s t	l s t	l s t	l s t	l s t	l s t	l s t	l s t	l s t	l s t
bag burp										

l = liquid output / s = semi-liquid/semi-thick / t = thick

symptom tracker

pain										
stress										
fatigue										
brain fog										
scale	1	2	3	4	5	6	7	8	9	10

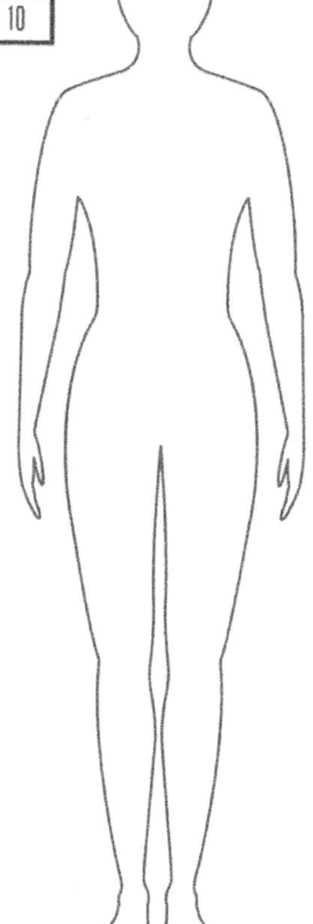

pain triggers

depression / anxiety / stress / no meds/ poor sleep / lack of activity / weather / overdid it

pain type and location:

achy / burning / stabbing / cramping / shooting / heavy / sharp / weak / throbbing

triggers (what made me happy, stressed etc.)	good things that happened	things that sucked

self-care

overall mood today:

DAILY CHECK-IN, PLANNER, AND TRACKER

DATE: M T W T F S S Month: __________ Day: __________

today's intention

today's challenges

wake time: ______ a.m. bedtime: ______ p.m.

hours slept: ______

how rested i feel:

😄 🙂 😕 ☹️ 😵

micro goals

priorities

optional

medication tracker	6am-10 am	10am-2pm	2pm-6pm	6pm-10pm	overnight
	additional:				

meal tracker

time	what i ate	how i felt

caffeine	
alcohol	
nicotine/vape	

physical activity

ostomy output tracker

bag changes										
bag empty/output	l s t	l s t	l s t	l s t	l s t	l s t	l s t	l s t	l s t	l s t
bag burp										

l = liquid output / s = semi-liquid/semi-thick / t = thick

symptom tracker

pain										
stress										
fatigue										
brain fog										
scale	1	2	3	4	5	6	7	8	9	10

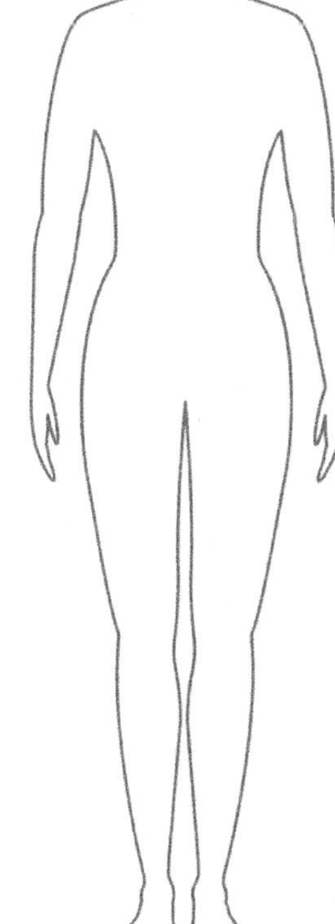

pain triggers

depression / anxiety / stress / no meds/ poor sleep / lack of activity / weather / overdid it

pain type and location:

achy / burning / stabbing / cramping / shooting / heavy / sharp / weak / throbbing

triggers
(what made me happy, stressed etc.)

good things that happened

things that sucked

self-care

overall mood today:

weekly review

week of: ______________

my successes:

what i accepted:

what i let go:

what i did for self-care:

what was better this week:

what was worse this week:

pain summary:

medication/
care changes:

weekly planner

week of: ____________

what i will do for self-care:

what i'm looking forward to most:

what i have to get through:

how i will cope:

what i want to accomplish this week:

DAILY CHECK-IN, PLANNER, AND TRACKER

DATE: M T W T F S S Month: __________ Day: __________

today's intention

today's challenges

wake time: ______ a.m. bedtime: ______ p.m.

hours slept: ______

how rested i feel:

micro goals

priorities

optional

medication tracker	6am-10 am	10am-2pm	2pm-6pm	6pm-10pm	overnight
	additional:				

meal tracker

time	what i ate	how i felt

caffeine	
alcohol	
nicotine/vape	

physical activity

ostomy output tracker

bag changes										
bag empty/output	l s t	l s t	l s t	l s t	l s t	l s t	l s t	l s t	l s t	l s t
bag burp										

l = liquid output / s = semi-liquid/semi-thick / t = thick

symptom tracker

pain										
stress										
fatigue										
brain fog										
scale	1	2	3	4	5	6	7	8	9	10

pain triggers

depression / anxiety / stress / no meds/ poor sleep / lack of activity / weather / overdid it

pain type and location:

achy / burning / stabbing / cramping / shooting / heavy / sharp / weak / throbbing

triggers
(what made me happy, stressed etc.)

good things that happened

things that sucked

self-care

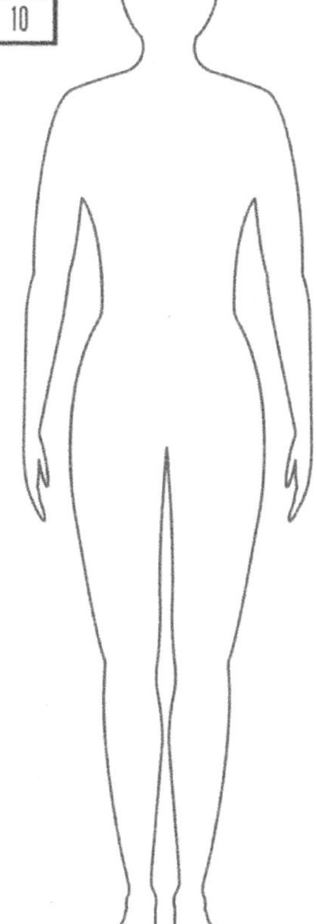

overall mood today:

DAILY CHECK-IN, PLANNER, AND TRACKER

DATE: M T W T F S S Month: ___________ Day: ___________

today's intention

today's challenges

wake time: ______ a.m. bedtime: ______ p.m.

hours slept: ______

how rested i feel:

micro goals

priorities

optional

medication tracker	6am-10 am	10am-2pm	2pm-6pm	6pm-10pm	overnight
	additional:				

meal tracker

time	what i ate	how i felt

caffeine	
alcohol	
nicotine/vape	

physical activity

ostomy output tracker

bag changes										
bag empty/output	l s t	l s t	l s t	l s t	l s t	l s t	l s t	l s t	l s t	l s t
bag burp										

l = liquid output / s = semi-liquid/semi-thick / t = thick

symptom tracker

pain										
stress										
fatigue										
brain fog										
scale	1	2	3	4	5	6	7	8	9	10

pain triggers

depression / anxiety / stress / no meds/ poor sleep / lack of activity / weather / overdid it

pain type and location:

achy / burning / stabbing / cramping / shooting / heavy / sharp / weak / throbbing

triggers
(what made me happy, stressed etc.)

good things that happened

things that sucked

self-care

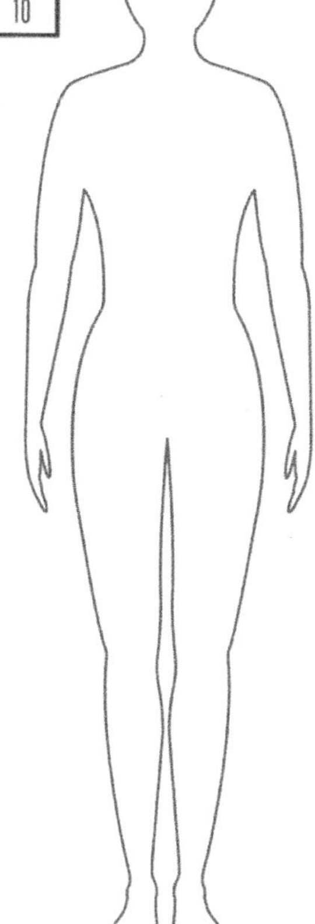

overall mood today:

DAILY CHECK-IN, PLANNER, AND TRACKER

DATE: M T W T F S S Month: __________ Day: __________

today's intention

today's challenges

wake time: ______ a.m. bedtime: ______ p.m.

hours slept: ______

how rested i feel:

micro goals	priorities	optional

medication tracker	6am-10 am	10am-2pm	2pm-6pm	6pm-10pm	overnight
	additional:				

meal tracker

time	what i ate	how i felt

caffeine	
alcohol	
nicotine/vape	

physical activity

ostomy output tracker

bag changes										
bag empty/output	l s t	l s t	l s t	l s t	l s t	l s t	l s t	l s t	l s t	l s t
bag burp										

l = liquid output / s = semi-liquid/semi-thick / t = thick

symptom tracker

pain										
stress										
fatigue										
brain fog										
scale	1	2	3	4	5	6	7	8	9	10

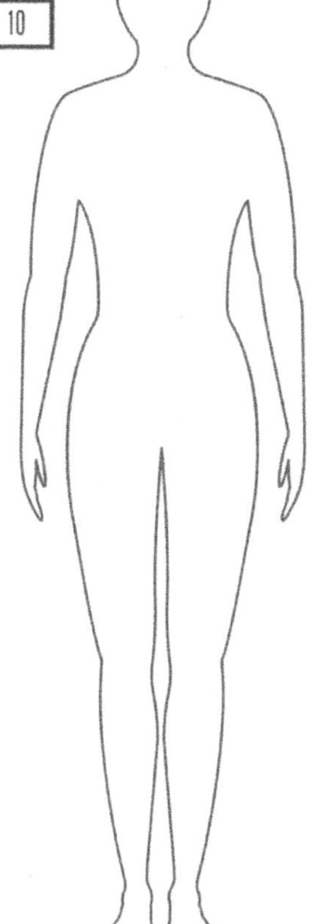

pain triggers

depression / anxiety / stress / no meds/ poor sleep / lack of activity / weather / overdid it

pain type and location:

achy / burning / stabbing / cramping / shooting / heavy / sharp / weak / throbbing

triggers (what made me happy, stressed etc.)	good things that happened	things that sucked

self-care

overall mood today:

DAILY CHECK-IN, PLANNER, AND TRACKER

DATE: M T W T F S S Month: __________ Day: __________

today's intention

today's challenges

wake time: ______ a.m. bedtime: ______ p.m.

hours slept: ______

how rested i feel:

😄 🙂 😕 ☹️ 😵

micro goals	priorities	optional

medication tracker	6am-10 am	10am-2pm	2pm-6pm	6pm-10pm	overnight
	additional:				

meal tracker

time	what i ate	how i felt

caffeine	
alcohol	
nicotine/vape	

physical activity

ostomy output tracker

bag changes										
bag empty/output	l s t	l s t	l s t	l s t	l s t	l s t	l s t	l s t	l s t	l s t
bag burp										

l = liquid output / s = semi-liquid/semi-thick / t = thick

symptom tracker

pain										
stress										
fatigue										
brain fog										
scale	1	2	3	4	5	6	7	8	9	10

pain triggers

depression / anxiety / stress / no meds/ poor sleep / lack of activity / weather / overdid it

pain type and location:

achy / burning / stabbing / cramping / shooting / heavy / sharp / weak / throbbing

triggers
(what made me happy, stressed etc.)

good things that happened

things that sucked

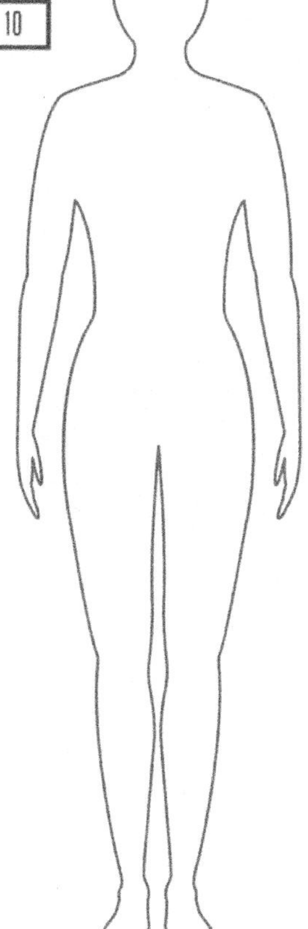

self-care

overall mood today:

DAILY CHECK-IN, PLANNER, AND TRACKER

DATE: M T W T F S S Month: __________ Day: __________

today's intention

today's challenges

wake time: ______ a.m. bedtime: ______ p.m.

hours slept: ______

how rested i feel:

micro goals

priorities

optional

medication tracker	6am-10 am	10am-2pm	2pm-6pm	6pm-10pm	overnight
	additional:				

meal tracker

time	what i ate	how i felt

caffeine	
alcohol	
nicotine/vape	

physical activity

ostomy output tracker

bag changes										
bag empty/output	l s t	l s t	l s t	l s t	l s t	l s t	l s t	l s t	l s t	l s t
bag burp										

l = liquid output / s = semi-liquid/semi-thick / t = thick

symptom tracker

pain										
stress										
fatigue										
brain fog										
scale	1	2	3	4	5	6	7	8	9	10

pain triggers

depression / anxiety / stress / no meds/ poor sleep / lack of activity / weather / overdid it

pain type and location:

achy / burning / stabbing / cramping / shooting / heavy / sharp / weak / throbbing

triggers
(what made me happy, stressed etc.)

good things that happened

things that sucked

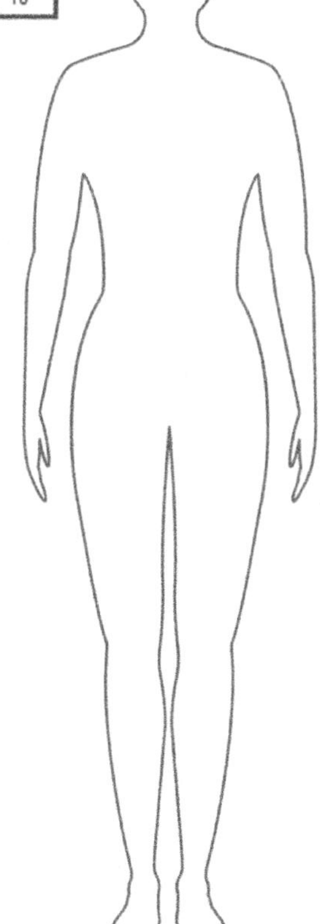

self-care

overall mood today:

DAILY CHECK-IN, PLANNER, AND TRACKER

DATE: M T W T F S S Month: ___________ Day: ___________

today's intention

today's challenges

wake time: ______ a.m. bedtime: ______ p.m.

hours slept: ______

how rested i feel:

micro goals	priorities	optional

medication tracker	6am-10 am	10am-2pm	2pm-6pm	6pm-10pm	overnight
	additional:				

meal tracker

time	what i ate	how i felt

caffeine	
alcohol	
nicotine/vape	

physical activity

ostomy output tracker

bag changes										
bag empty/output	l s t	l s t	l s t	l s t	l s t	l s t	l s t	l s t	l s t	l s t
bag burp										

l = liquid output / s = semi-liquid/semi-thick / t = thick

symptom tracker

pain										
stress										
fatigue										
brain fog										
scale	1	2	3	4	5	6	7	8	9	10

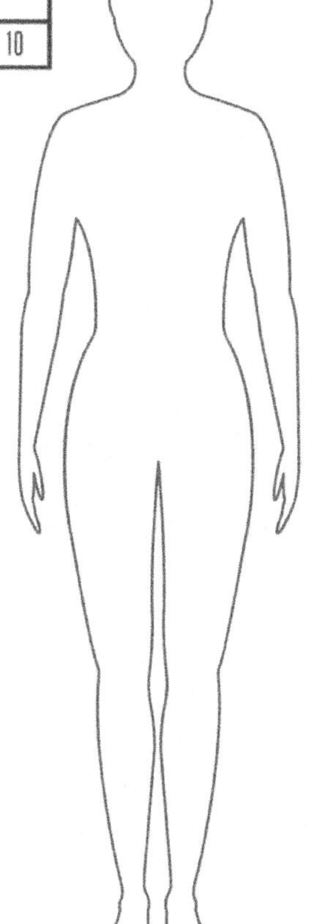

pain triggers

depression / anxiety / stress / no meds/ poor sleep / lack of activity / weather / overdid it

pain type and location:

achy / burning / stabbing / cramping / shooting / heavy / sharp / weak / throbbing

triggers
(what made me happy, stressed etc.)

good things that happened

things that sucked

self-care

overall mood today:

DAILY CHECK-IN, PLANNER, AND TRACKER

DATE: M T W T F S S Month: ___________ Day: ___________

today's intention

today's challenges

wake time: _______ a.m. bedtime: _______ p.m.

hours slept: _______

how rested i feel:

micro goals

priorities

optional

medication tracker	6am-10 am	10am-2pm	2pm-6pm	6pm-10pm	overnight
	additional:				

meal tracker

time	what i ate	how i felt

caffeine	
alcohol	
nicotine/vape	

physical activity

ostomy output tracker

bag changes										
bag empty/output	l s t	l s t	l s t	l s t	l s t	l s t	l s t	l s t	l s t	l s t
bag burp										

l = liquid output / s = semi-liquid/semi-thick / t = thick

symptom tracker

pain										
stress										
fatigue										
brain fog										
scale	1	2	3	4	5	6	7	8	9	10

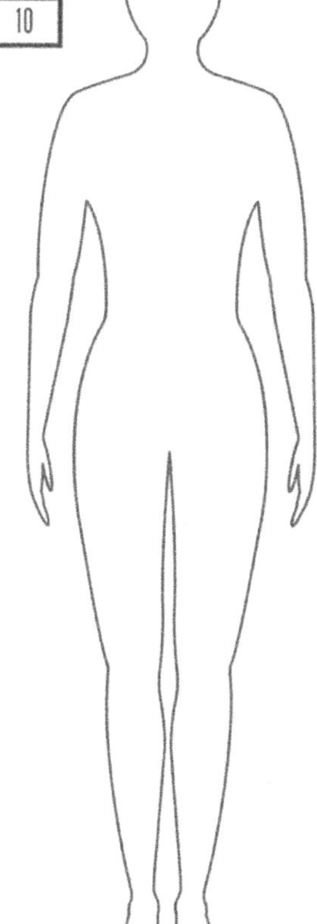

pain triggers

depression / anxiety / stress / no meds/ poor sleep / lack of activity / weather / overdid it

pain type and location:

achy / burning / stabbing / cramping / shooting / heavy / sharp / weak / throbbing

triggers
(what made me happy, stressed etc.)

good things that happened

things that sucked

self-care

overall mood today:

weekly review

week of: ____________________

my successes:

what i accepted:

what i let go:

what i did for self-care:

what was better this week:

what was worse this week:

pain summary:

medication/
care changes:

weekly planner

week of: ____________

what i will do for self-care:

what i'm looking forward to most:

what i have to get through:

how i will cope:

what i want to accomplish this week:

DAILY CHECK-IN, PLANNER, AND TRACKER

DATE: M T W T F S S Month: ___________ Day: ___________

today's intention

today's challenges

wake time: _______ a.m. bedtime: _______ p.m.

hours slept: _______

how rested i feel:

micro goals	priorities	optional

medication tracker	6am-10 am	10am-2pm	2pm-6pm	6pm-10pm	overnight
	additional:				

meal tracker

time	what i ate	how i felt

caffeine	
alcohol	
nicotine/vape	

physical activity

ostomy output tracker

bag changes										
bag empty/output	l s t	l s t	l s t	l s t	l s t	l s t	l s t	l s t	l s t	l s t
bag burp										

l = liquid output / s = semi-liquid/semi-thick / t = thick

symptom tracker

pain										
stress										
fatigue										
brain fog										
scale	1	2	3	4	5	6	7	8	9	10

pain triggers

depression / anxiety / stress / no meds/ poor sleep / lack of activity / weather / overdid it

pain type and location:

achy / burning / stabbing / cramping / shooting / heavy / sharp / weak / throbbing

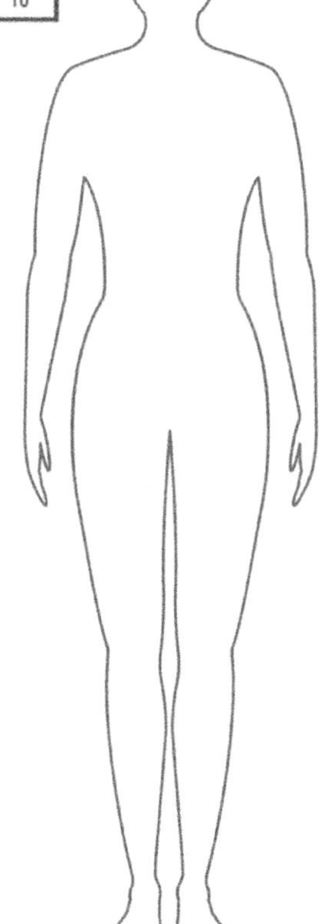

triggers
(what made me happy, stressed etc.)

good things that happened

things that sucked

self-care

overall mood today:

DAILY CHECK-IN, PLANNER, AND TRACKER

DATE: M T W T F S S Month: ___________ Day: ___________

today's intention

today's challenges

wake time: _______ a.m. bedtime: _______ p.m.

hours slept: _______

how rested i feel:

😄 🙂 😕 ☹️ 😵

micro goals	priorities	optional

medication tracker	6am-10 am	10am-2pm	2pm-6pm	6pm-10pm	overnight
	additional:				

meal tracker

time	what i ate	how i felt

caffeine	
alcohol	
nicotine/vape	

physical activity

ostomy output tracker

bag changes										
bag empty/output	l s t	l s t	l s t	l s t	l s t	l s t	l s t	l s t	l s t	l s t
bag burp										

l = liquid output / s = semi-liquid/semi-thick / t = thick

symptom tracker

pain										
stress										
fatigue										
brain fog										
scale	1	2	3	4	5	6	7	8	9	10

pain triggers

depression / anxiety / stress / no meds/ poor sleep / lack of activity / weather / overdid it

pain type and location:

achy / burning / stabbing / cramping / shooting / heavy / sharp / weak / throbbing

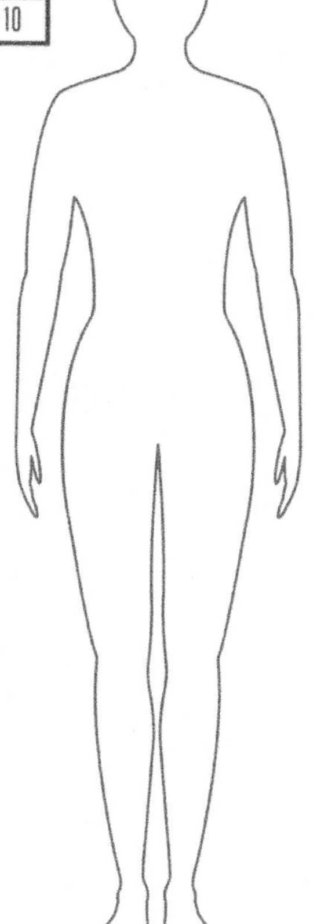

triggers
(what made me happy, stressed etc.)

good things that happened

things that sucked

self-care

overall mood today:

DAILY CHECK-IN, PLANNER, AND TRACKER

DATE: M T W T F S S Month: __________ Day: __________

today's intention

today's challenges

wake time: ______ a.m. bedtime: ______ p.m.

hours slept: ______

how rested i feel:

😄 🙂 😕 ☹️ 😵

micro goals

priorities

optional

medication tracker	6am-10 am	10am-2pm	2pm-6pm	6pm-10pm	overnight
	additional:				

meal tracker

time	what i ate	how i felt

caffeine	
alcohol	
nicotine/vape	

physical activity

ostomy output tracker

bag changes										
bag empty/output	l s t	l s t	l s t	l s t	l s t	l s t	l s t	l s t	l s t	l s t
bag burp										

l = liquid output / s = semi-liquid/semi-thick / t = thick

symptom tracker

pain										
stress										
fatigue										
brain fog										
scale	1	2	3	4	5	6	7	8	9	10

pain triggers

depression / anxiety / stress / no meds/ poor sleep / lack of activity / weather / overdid it

pain type and location:

achy / burning / stabbing / cramping / shooting / heavy / sharp / weak / throbbing

triggers
(what made me happy, stressed etc.)

good things that happened

things that sucked

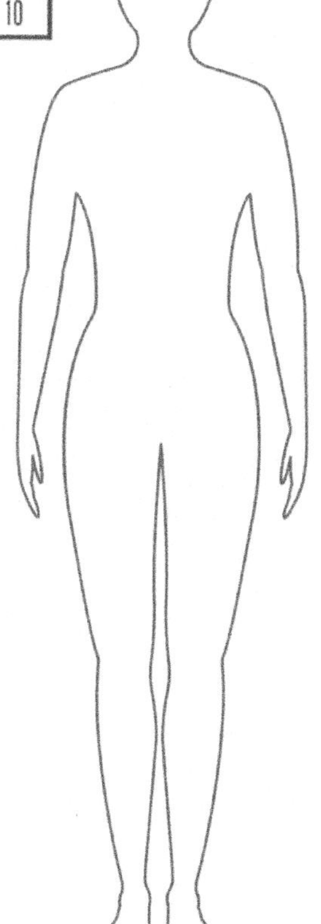

self-care

overall mood today:

DAILY CHECK-IN, PLANNER, AND TRACKER

DATE: M T W T F S S Month: ___________ Day: ___________

today's intention

today's challenges

wake time: ______ a.m. bedtime: ______ p.m.

hours slept: ______

how rested i feel:

micro goals

priorities

optional

medication tracker	6am-10 am	10am-2pm	2pm-6pm	6pm-10pm	overnight
	additional:				

meal tracker

time	what i ate	how i felt

caffeine	
alcohol	
nicotine/vape	

physical activity

ostomy output tracker

bag changes										
bag empty/output	l s t	l s t	l s t	l s t	l s t	l s t	l s t	l s t	l s t	l s t
bag burp										

l = liquid output / s = semi-liquid/semi-thick / t = thick

symptom tracker

pain										
stress										
fatigue										
brain fog										
scale	1	2	3	4	5	6	7	8	9	10

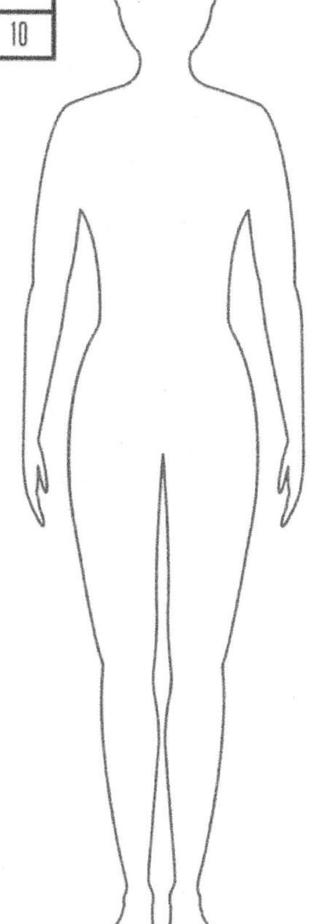

pain triggers

depression / anxiety / stress / no meds/ poor sleep / lack of activity / weather / overdid it

pain type and location:

achy / burning / stabbing / cramping / shooting / heavy / sharp / weak / throbbing

triggers
(what made me happy, stressed etc.)

good things that happened

things that sucked

self-care

overall mood today:

DAILY CHECK-IN, PLANNER, AND TRACKER

DATE: M T W T F S S Month: ___________ Day: ___________

today's intention

today's challenges

wake time: ______ a.m. bedtime: ______ p.m.

hours slept: ______

how rested i feel:

micro goals

priorities

optional

medication tracker	6am-10 am	10am-2pm	2pm-6pm	6pm-10pm	overnight
	additional:				

meal tracker

time	what i ate	how i felt

caffeine	
alcohol	
nicotine/vape	

physical activity

ostomy output tracker

bag changes										
bag empty/output	l s t	l s t	l s t	l s t	l s t	l s t	l s t	l s t	l s t	l s t
bag burp										

l = liquid output / s = semi-liquid/semi-thick / t = thick

symptom tracker

pain										
stress										
fatigue										
brain fog										
scale	1	2	3	4	5	6	7	8	9	10

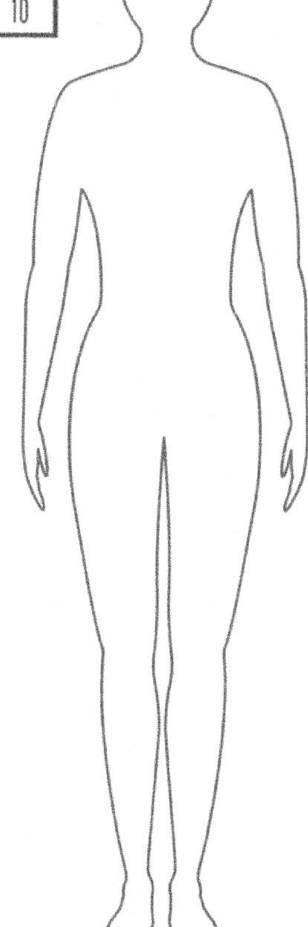

pain triggers

depression / anxiety / stress / no meds/ poor sleep / lack of activity / weather / overdid it

pain type and location:

achy / burning / stabbing / cramping / shooting / heavy / sharp / weak / throbbing

triggers (what made me happy, stressed etc.)	good things that happened	things that sucked

self-care

overall mood today:

DAILY CHECK-IN, PLANNER, AND TRACKER

DATE: M T W T F S S Month: __________ Day: __________

today's intention

today's challenges

wake time: ______ a.m. bedtime: ______ p.m.

hours slept: ______

how rested i feel:

micro goals

priorities

optional

medication tracker	6am-10 am	10am-2pm	2pm-6pm	6pm-10pm	overnight
	additional:				

meal tracker

time	what i ate	how i felt

caffeine	
alcohol	
nicotine/vape	

physical activity

ostomy output tracker

bag changes										
bag empty/output	l s t	l s t	l s t	l s t	l s t	l s t	l s t	l s t	l s t	l s t
bag burp										

l = liquid output / s = semi-liquid/semi-thick / t = thick

symptom tracker

pain										
stress										
fatigue										
brain fog										
scale	1	2	3	4	5	6	7	8	9	10

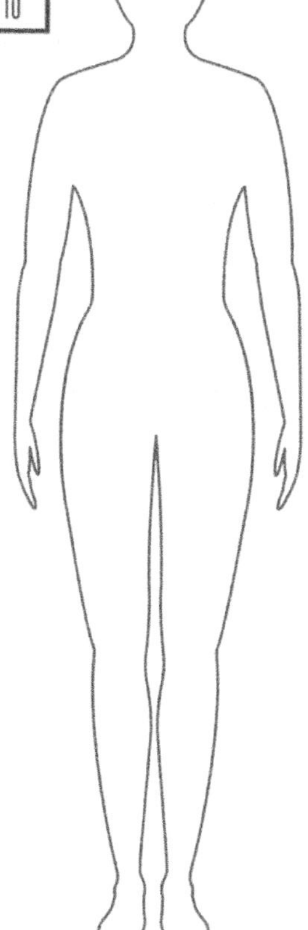

pain triggers

depression / anxiety / stress / no meds/ poor sleep / lack of activity / weather / overdid it

pain type and location:

achy / burning / stabbing / cramping / shooting / heavy / sharp / weak / throbbing

triggers
(what made me happy, stressed etc.)

good things that happened

things that sucked

self-care

overall mood today:

DAILY CHECK-IN, PLANNER, AND TRACKER

DATE: M T W T F S S Month: __________ Day: __________

today's intention

today's challenges

wake time: ______ a.m. bedtime: ______ p.m.

hours slept: ______

how rested i feel:

😄 🙂 😕 ☹️ 😵

micro goals	priorities	optional

medication tracker	6am-10 am	10am-2pm	2pm-6pm	6pm-10pm	overnight
	additional:				

meal tracker

time	what i ate	how i felt

caffeine	
alcohol	
nicotine/vape	

physical activity

ostomy output tracker

bag changes										
bag empty/output	l s t	l s t	l s t	l s t	l s t	l s t	l s t	l s t	l s t	l s t
bag burp										

l = liquid output / s = semi-liquid/semi-thick / t = thick

symptom tracker

pain										
stress										
fatigue										
brain fog										
scale	1	2	3	4	5	6	7	8	9	10

pain triggers

depression / anxiety / stress / no meds/ poor sleep / lack of activity / weather / overdid it

pain type and location:

achy / burning / stabbing / cramping / shooting / heavy / sharp / weak / throbbing

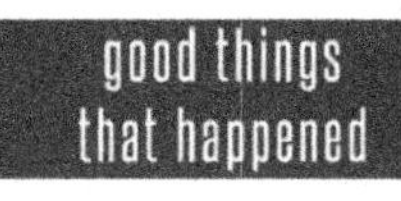

triggers (what made me happy, stressed etc.)	good things that happened	things that sucked

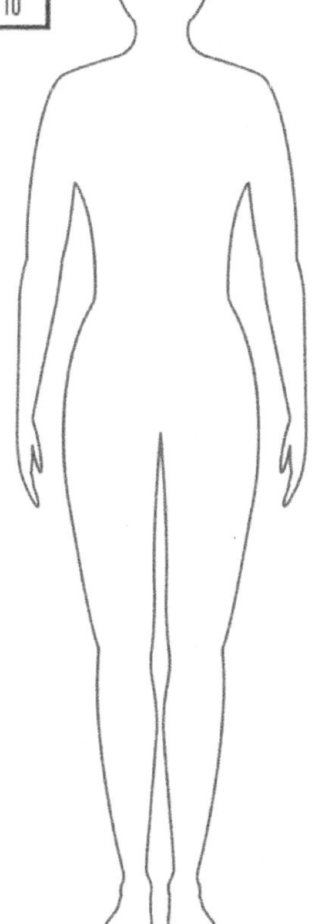

self-care

overall mood today:

weekly review

week of: ____________________

my successes:

what i accepted:

what i let go:

what i did for self-care:

what was better this week:

what was worse this week:

pain summary:

medication/
care changes:

weekly planner

week of: ______________

what i will do for self-care:

what i'm looking forward to most:

what i have to get through:

how i will cope:

what i want to accomplish this week:

DAILY CHECK-IN, PLANNER, AND TRACKER

DATE: M T W T F S S Month: ___________ Day: ___________

today's intention

today's challenges

wake time: _______ a.m. bedtime: _______ p.m.

hours slept: _______

how rested i feel:

micro goals	priorities	optional

medication tracker	6am-10 am	10am-2pm	2pm-6pm	6pm-10pm	overnight
	additional:				

meal tracker

time	what i ate	how i felt

caffeine	
alcohol	
nicotine/vape	

physical activity

ostomy output tracker

bag changes										
bag empty/output	l s t	l s t	l s t	l s t	l s t	l s t	l s t	l s t	l s t	l s t
bag burp										

l = liquid output / s = semi-liquid/semi-thick / t = thick

symptom tracker

pain										
stress										
fatigue										
brain fog										
scale	1	2	3	4	5	6	7	8	9	10

pain triggers

depression / anxiety / stress / no meds/ poor sleep / lack of activity / weather / overdid it

pain type and location:

achy / burning / stabbing / cramping / shooting / heavy / sharp / weak / throbbing

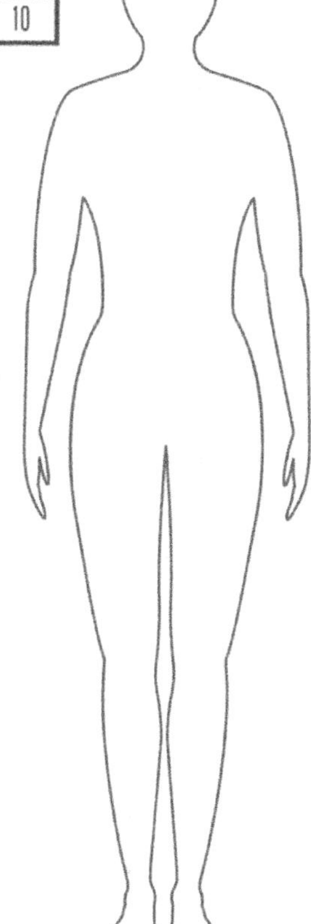

triggers
(what made me happy, stressed etc.)

good things that happened

things that sucked

self-care

overall mood today:

DAILY CHECK-IN, PLANNER, AND TRACKER

DATE: M T W T F S S Month: __________ Day: __________

today's intention

today's challenges

wake time: ______ a.m. bedtime: ______ p.m.

hours slept: ______

how rested i feel:

micro goals

priorities

optional

medication tracker	6am-10 am	10am-2pm	2pm-6pm	6pm-10pm	overnight
	additional:				

meal tracker

time	what i ate	how i felt

caffeine	
alcohol	
nicotine/vape	

physical activity

ostomy output tracker

bag changes										
bag empty/output	l s t	l s t	l s t	l s t	l s t	l s t	l s t	l s t	l s t	l s t
bag burp										

l = liquid output / s = semi-liquid/semi-thick / t = thick

symptom tracker

pain										
stress										
fatigue										
brain fog										
scale	1	2	3	4	5	6	7	8	9	10

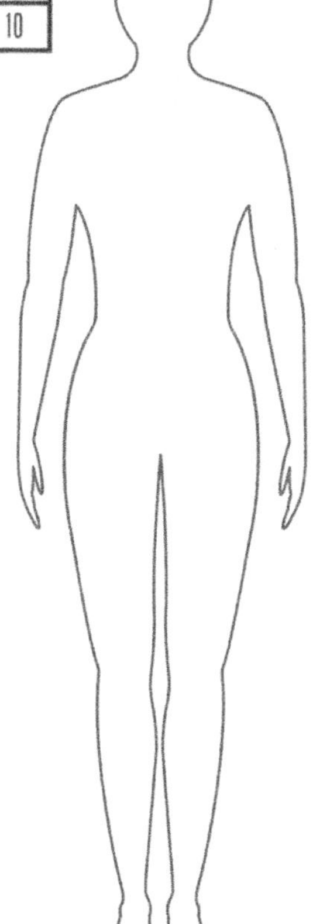

pain triggers

depression / anxiety / stress / no meds/ poor sleep / lack of activity / weather / overdid it

pain type and location:

achy / burning / stabbing / cramping / shooting / heavy / sharp / weak / throbbing

triggers
(what made me happy, stressed etc.)

good things that happened

things that sucked

self-care

overall mood today:

DAILY CHECK-IN, PLANNER, AND TRACKER

DATE: M T W T F S S Month: ___________ Day: ___________

today's intention

today's challenges

wake time: ______ a.m. bedtime: ______ p.m.

hours slept: ______

how rested i feel:

micro goals

priorities

optional

medication tracker	6am-10 am	10am-2pm	2pm-6pm	6pm-10pm	overnight
	additional:				

meal tracker

time	what i ate	how i felt

caffeine	
alcohol	
nicotine/vape	

physical activity

ostomy output tracker

bag changes										
bag empty/output	l s t	l s t	l s t	l s t	l s t	l s t	l s t	l s t	l s t	l s t
bag burp										

l = liquid output / s = semi-liquid/semi-thick / t = thick

symptom tracker

pain										
stress										
fatigue										
brain fog										
scale	1	2	3	4	5	6	7	8	9	10

pain triggers

depression / anxiety / stress / no meds/ poor sleep / lack of activity / weather / overdid it

pain type and location:

achy / burning / stabbing / cramping / shooting / heavy / sharp / weak / throbbing

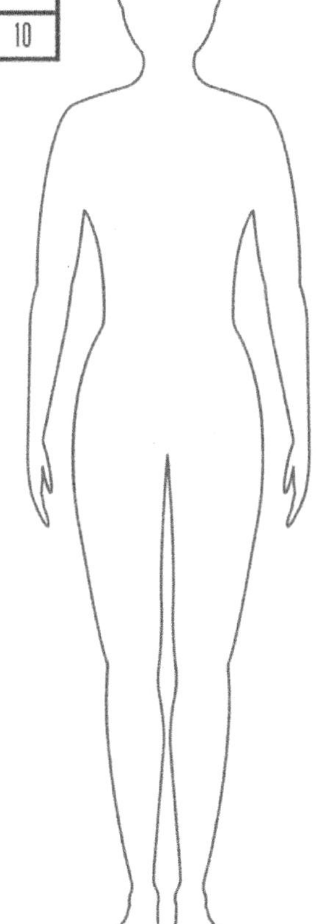

triggers
(what made me happy, stressed etc.)

good things that happened

things that sucked

self-care

overall mood today:

weekly review

week of: ____________________

my successes:

what i accepted:

what i let go:

what i did for self-care:

what was better this week:

what was worse this week:

pain summary:

medication/
care changes:

monthly review

month: ______________

my successes:

what i accepted:

what i let go:

what i did for self-care:

what was better this month:

what was worse this month:

pain summary:

medication/
care changes:

notes:

monthly planner

month: ____________

what i will do for self-care:

what i'm looking forward to most:

what i have to get through:

how i will cope:

what i want to accomplish this month:

appointment tracker

date	time	doctor	location	issue	outcome

current medications

name	dose	times per day/week/month	side effects	refill on:

new treatment/medication:

weekly planner

week of: ____________

what i will do for self-care:

what i'm looking forward to most:

what i have to get through:

how i will cope:

what i want to accomplish this week:

DAILY CHECK-IN, PLANNER, AND TRACKER

DATE: M T W T F S S Month: __________ Day: __________

today's intention

today's challenges

wake time: ______ a.m. bedtime: ______ p.m.

hours slept: ______

how rested i feel:

micro goals

priorities

optional

medication tracker	6am-10 am	10am-2pm	2pm-6pm	6pm-10pm	overnight
	additional:				

meal tracker

time	what i ate	how i felt

caffeine	
alcohol	
nicotine/vape	

physical activity

ostomy output tracker

bag changes										
bag empty/output	l s t	l s t	l s t	l s t	l s t	l s t	l s t	l s t	l s t	l s t
bag burp										

l = liquid output / s = semi-liquid/semi-thick / t = thick

symptom tracker

pain										
stress										
fatigue										
brain fog										
scale	1	2	3	4	5	6	7	8	9	10

pain triggers

depression / anxiety / stress / no meds/ poor sleep / lack of activity / weather / overdid it

pain type and location:

achy / burning / stabbing / cramping / shooting / heavy / sharp / weak / throbbing

triggers
(what made me happy, stressed etc.)

good things that happened

things that sucked

self-care

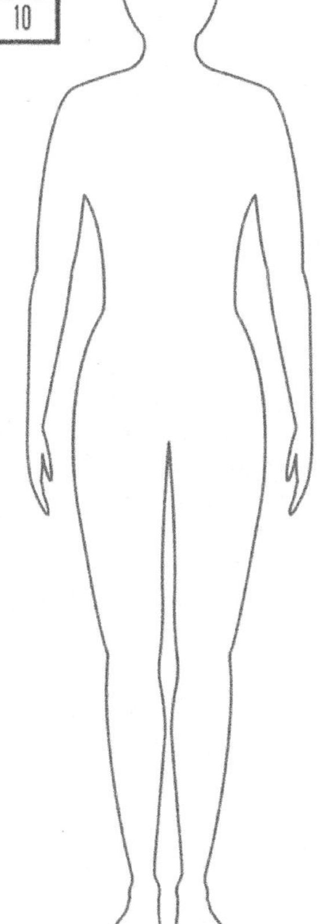

overall mood today:

DAILY CHECK-IN, PLANNER, AND TRACKER

DATE: M T W T F S S Month: ___________ Day: ___________

today's intention

today's challenges

wake time: _______ a.m. bedtime: _______ p.m.

hours slept: _______

how rested i feel:

micro goals

priorities

optional

medication tracker	6am-10 am	10am-2pm	2pm-6pm	6pm-10pm	overnight
	additional:				

meal tracker

time	what i ate	how i felt

caffeine	
alcohol	
nicotine/vape	

physical activity

ostomy output tracker

bag changes										
bag empty/output	l s t	l s t	l s t	l s t	l s t	l s t	l s t	l s t	l s t	l s t
bag burp										

l = liquid output / s = semi-liquid/semi-thick / t = thick

symptom tracker

pain										
stress										
fatigue										
brain fog										
scale	1	2	3	4	5	6	7	8	9	10

pain triggers

depression / anxiety / stress / no meds/ poor sleep / lack of activity / weather / overdid it

pain type and location:

achy / burning / stabbing / cramping / shooting / heavy / sharp / weak / throbbing

triggers
(what made me happy, stressed etc.)

good things that happened

things that sucked

self-care

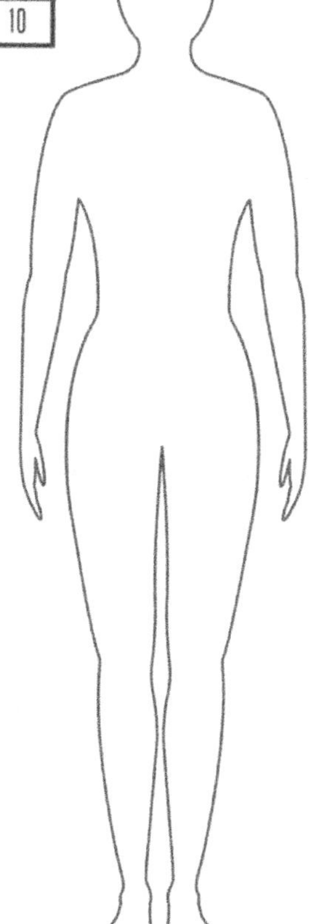

overall mood today:

DAILY CHECK-IN, PLANNER, AND TRACKER

DATE: M T W T F S S Month: ___________ Day: ___________

today's intention

today's challenges

wake time: ______ a.m. bedtime: ______ p.m.

hours slept: ______

how rested i feel:

micro goals

priorities

optional

medication tracker	6am-10 am	10am-2pm	2pm-6pm	6pm-10pm	overnight
	additional:				

meal tracker

time	what i ate	how i felt

caffeine	
alcohol	
nicotine/vape	

physical activity

ostomy output tracker

bag changes										
bag empty/output	l s t	l s t	l s t	l s t	l s t	l s t	l s t	l s t	l s t	l s t
bag burp										

l = liquid output / s = semi-liquid/semi-thick / t = thick

symptom tracker

pain										
stress										
fatigue										
brain fog										
scale	1	2	3	4	5	6	7	8	9	10

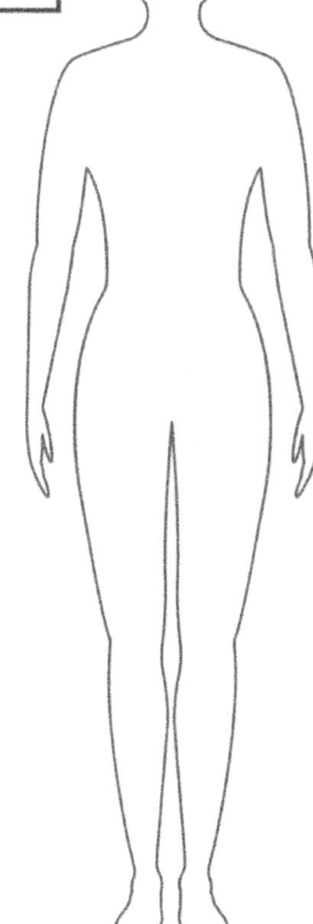

pain triggers

depression / anxiety / stress / no meds/ poor sleep / lack of activity / weather / overdid it

pain type and location:

achy / burning / stabbing / cramping / shooting / heavy / sharp / weak / throbbing

triggers (what made me happy, stressed etc.)	good things that happened	things that sucked

self-care

overall mood today:

DAILY CHECK-IN, PLANNER, AND TRACKER

DATE: M T W T F S S Month: __________ Day: __________

today's intention

today's challenges

wake time: ______ a.m. bedtime: ______ p.m.

hours slept: ______

how rested i feel:

micro goals

priorities

optional

medication tracker	6am-10 am	10am-2pm	2pm-6pm	6pm-10pm	overnight
	additional:				

meal tracker

time	what i ate	how i felt

caffeine	
alcohol	
nicotine/vape	

physical activity

ostomy output tracker

bag changes										
bag empty/output	l s t	l s t	l s t	l s t	l s t	l s t	l s t	l s t	l s t	l s t
bag burp										

l = liquid output / s = semi-liquid/semi-thick / t = thick

symptom tracker

pain										
stress										
fatigue										
brain fog										
scale	1	2	3	4	5	6	7	8	9	10

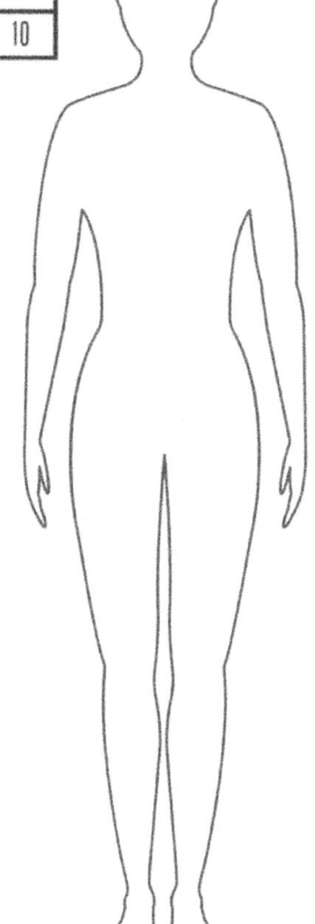

pain triggers

depression / anxiety / stress / no meds/ poor sleep / lack of activity / weather / overdid it

pain type and location:

achy / burning / stabbing / cramping / shooting / heavy / sharp / weak / throbbing

triggers
(what made me happy, stressed etc.)

good things that happened

things that sucked

self-care

overall mood today:

DAILY CHECK-IN, PLANNER, AND TRACKER

DATE: M T W T F S S Month: ___________ Day: ___________

today's intention

today's challenges

wake time: _______ a.m. bedtime: _______ p.m.

hours slept: _______

how rested i feel:

micro goals	priorities	optional

medication tracker	6am-10 am	10am-2pm	2pm-6pm	6pm-10pm	overnight
	additional:				

meal tracker

time	what i ate	how i felt

caffeine	
alcohol	
nicotine/vape	

physical activity

ostomy output tracker

bag changes										
bag empty/output	l s t	l s t	l s t	l s t	l s t	l s t	l s t	l s t	l s t	l s t
bag burp										

l = liquid output / s = semi-liquid/semi-thick / t = thick

symptom tracker

pain										
stress										
fatigue										
brain fog										
scale	1	2	3	4	5	6	7	8	9	10

pain triggers

depression / anxiety / stress / no meds/ poor sleep / lack of activity / weather / overdid it

pain type and location:

achy / burning / stabbing / cramping / shooting / heavy / sharp / weak / throbbing

triggers
(what made me happy, stressed etc.)

good things that happened

things that sucked

self-care

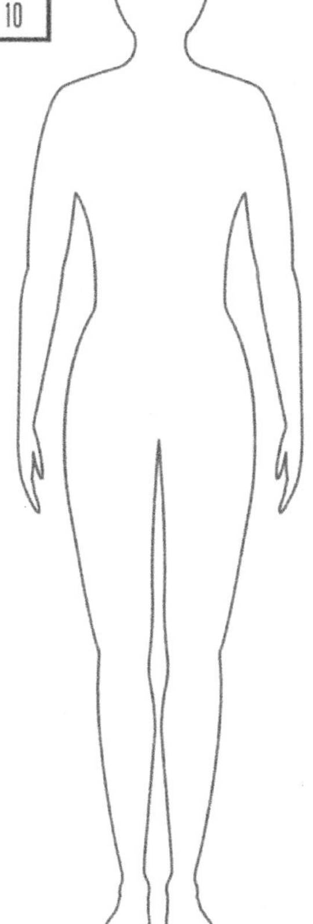

overall mood today:

DAILY CHECK-IN, PLANNER, AND TRACKER

DATE: M T W T F S S Month: __________ Day: __________

today's intention

today's challenges

wake time: _______ a.m. bedtime: _______ p.m.

hours slept: _______

how rested i feel:

😄 🙂 😕 ☹️ 😵

micro goals	priorities	optional

medication tracker	6am-10 am	10am-2pm	2pm-6pm	6pm-10pm	overnight
	additional:				

meal tracker

time	what i ate	how i felt

caffeine	
alcohol	
nicotine/vape	

physical activity

ostomy output tracker

bag changes										
bag empty/output	l s t	l s t	l s t	l s t	l s t	l s t	l s t	l s t	l s t	l s t
bag burp										

l = liquid output / s = semi-liquid/semi-thick / t = thick

symptom tracker

pain										
stress										
fatigue										
brain fog										
scale	1	2	3	4	5	6	7	8	9	10

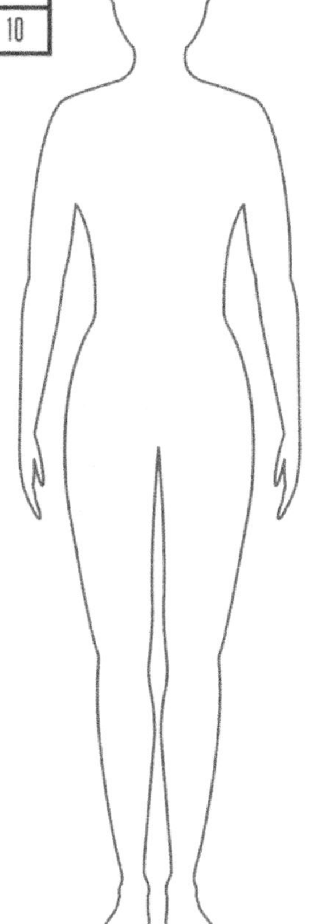

pain triggers

depression / anxiety / stress / no meds/ poor sleep / lack of activity / weather / overdid it

pain type and location:

achy / burning / stabbing / cramping / shooting / heavy / sharp / weak / throbbing

triggers
(what made me happy, stressed etc.)

good things that happened

things that sucked

self-care

overall mood today:

DAILY CHECK-IN, PLANNER, AND TRACKER

DATE: M T W T F S S Month: __________ Day: __________

today's intention

today's challenges

wake time: ______ a.m. bedtime: ______ p.m.

hours slept: ______

how rested i feel:

micro goals

priorities

optional

medication tracker	6am-10 am	10am-2pm	2pm-6pm	6pm-10pm	overnight
	additional:				

meal tracker

time	what i ate	how i felt

caffeine	
alcohol	
nicotine/vape	

physical activity

ostomy output tracker

bag changes										
bag empty/output	l s t	l s t	l s t	l s t	l s t	l s t	l s t	l s t	l s t	l s t
bag burp										

l = liquid output / s = semi-liquid/semi-thick / t = thick

symptom tracker

pain										
stress										
fatigue										
brain fog										
scale	1	2	3	4	5	6	7	8	9	10

pain triggers

depression / anxiety / stress / no meds/ poor sleep / lack of activity / weather / overdid it

pain type and location:

achy / burning / stabbing / cramping / shooting / heavy / sharp / weak / throbbing

triggers
(what made me happy, stressed etc.)

good things that happened

things that sucked

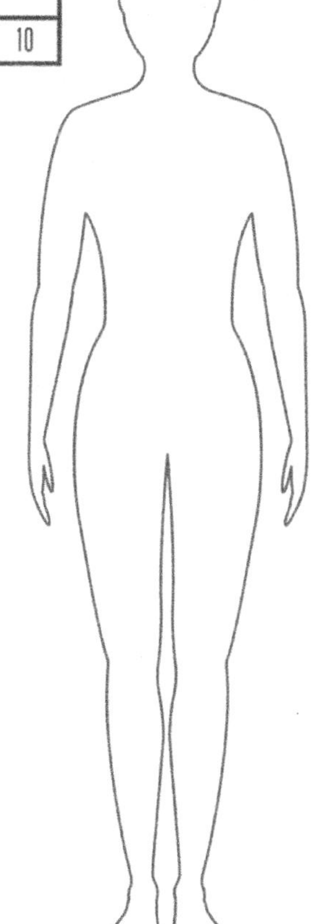

self-care

overall mood today:

weekly review

week of: ____________________

my successes:

what i accepted:

what i let go:

what i did for self-care:

what was better this week:

what was worse this week:

pain summary:

medication/ care changes:

weekly planner

week of: ____________

what i will do for self-care:

what i'm looking forward to most:

what i have to get through:

how i will cope:

what i want to accomplish this week:

DAILY CHECK-IN, PLANNER, AND TRACKER

DATE: M T W T F S S Month: __________ Day: __________

today's intention

today's challenges

wake time: ______ a.m. bedtime: ______ p.m.

hours slept: ______

how rested i feel:

micro goals	priorities	optional

medication tracker	6am-10 am	10am-2pm	2pm-6pm	6pm-10pm	overnight
	additional:				

meal tracker

time	what i ate	how i felt

caffeine	
alcohol	
nicotine/vape	

physical activity

ostomy output tracker

bag changes										
bag empty/output	l s t	l s t	l s t	l s t	l s t	l s t	l s t	l s t	l s t	l s t
bag burp										

l = liquid output / s = semi-liquid/semi-thick / t = thick

symptom tracker

pain										
stress										
fatigue										
brain fog										
scale	1	2	3	4	5	6	7	8	9	10

pain triggers

depression / anxiety / stress / no meds/ poor sleep / lack of activity / weather / overdid it

pain type and location:

achy / burning / stabbing / cramping / shooting / heavy / sharp / weak / throbbing

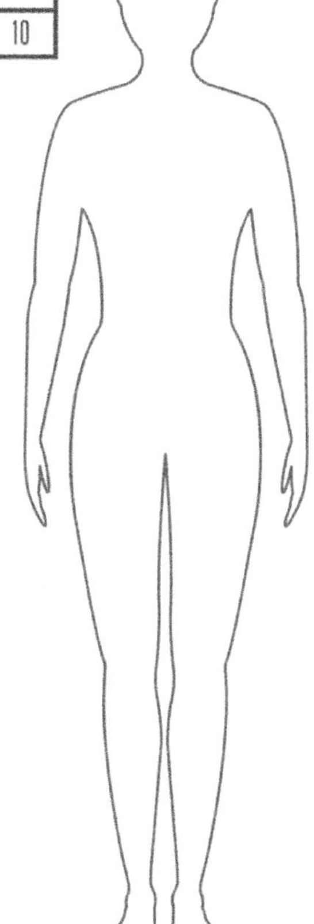

triggers
(what made me happy, stressed etc.)

good things that happened

things that sucked

self-care

overall mood today:

DAILY CHECK-IN, PLANNER, AND TRACKER

DATE: M T W T F S S Month: ____________ Day: ____________

today's intention

today's challenges

wake time: ________ a.m. bedtime: ________ p.m.

hours slept: ________

how rested i feel:

micro goals

priorities

optional

medication tracker	6am-10 am	10am-2pm	2pm-6pm	6pm-10pm	overnight
	additional:				

meal tracker

time	what i ate	how i felt

caffeine	
alcohol	
nicotine/vape	

physical activity

ostomy output tracker

bag changes										
bag empty/output	l s t	l s t	l s t	l s t	l s t	l s t	l s t	l s t	l s t	l s t
bag burp										

l = liquid output / s = semi-liquid/semi-thick / t = thick

symptom tracker

pain										
stress										
fatigue										
brain fog										
scale	1	2	3	4	5	6	7	8	9	10

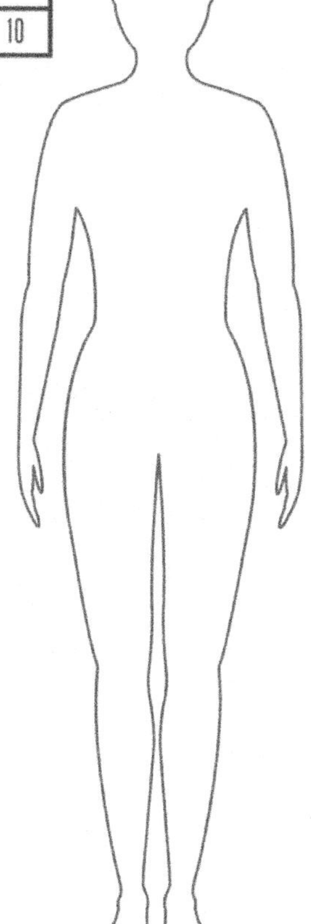

pain triggers

depression / anxiety / stress / no meds/ poor sleep / lack of activity / weather / overdid it

pain type and location:

achy / burning / stabbing / cramping / shooting / heavy / sharp / weak / throbbing

triggers
(what made me happy, stressed etc.)

good things that happened

things that sucked

self-care

overall mood today:

DAILY CHECK-IN, PLANNER, AND TRACKER

DATE: M T W T F S S Month: __________ Day: __________

today's intention

today's challenges

wake time: ______ a.m. bedtime: ______ p.m.

hours slept: ______

how rested i feel:

😄 🙂 😕 ☹️ 😵

micro goals	priorities	optional

medication tracker	6am-10 am	10am-2pm	2pm-6pm	6pm-10pm	overnight
	additional:				

meal tracker

time	what i ate	how i felt

caffeine	
alcohol	
nicotine/vape	

physical activity

ostomy output tracker

bag changes										
bag empty/output	l s t	l s t	l s t	l s t	l s t	l s t	l s t	l s t	l s t	l s t
bag burp										

l = liquid output / s = semi-liquid/semi-thick / t = thick

symptom tracker

pain										
stress										
fatigue										
brain fog										
scale	1	2	3	4	5	6	7	8	9	10

pain triggers

depression / anxiety / stress / no meds/ poor sleep / lack of activity / weather / overdid it

pain type and location:

achy / burning / stabbing / cramping / shooting / heavy / sharp / weak / throbbing

triggers
(what made me happy, stressed etc.)

good things that happened

things that sucked

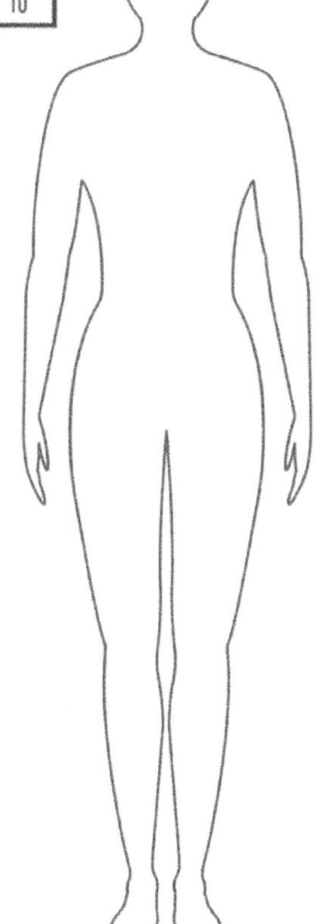

self-care

overall mood today:

DAILY CHECK-IN, PLANNER, AND TRACKER

DATE: M T W T F S S Month: ___________ Day: ___________

today's intention

today's challenges

wake time: ______ a.m. bedtime: ______ p.m.

hours slept: ______

how rested i feel:

micro goals

priorities

optional

medication tracker	6am-10 am	10am-2pm	2pm-6pm	6pm-10pm	overnight
	additional:				

meal tracker

time	what i ate	how i felt

caffeine	
alcohol	
nicotine/vape	

physical activity

ostomy output tracker

bag changes										
bag empty/output	l s t	l s t	l s t	l s t	l s t	l s t	l s t	l s t	l s t	l s t
bag burp										

l = liquid output / s = semi-liquid/semi-thick / t = thick

symptom tracker

pain										
stress										
fatigue										
brain fog										
scale	1	2	3	4	5	6	7	8	9	10

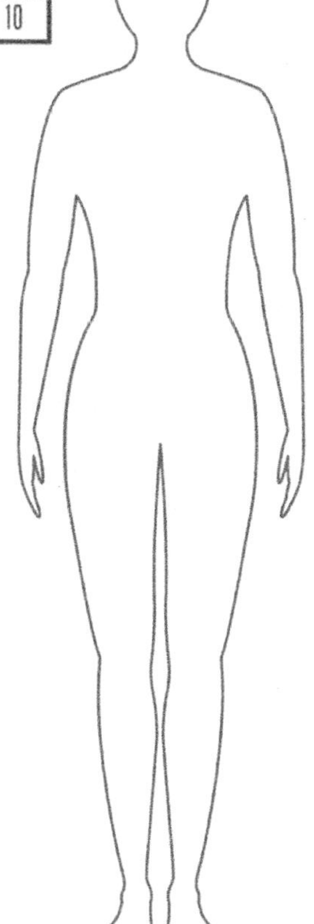

pain triggers

depression / anxiety / stress / no meds/ poor sleep / lack of activity / weather / overdid it

pain type and location:

achy / burning / stabbing / cramping / shooting / heavy / sharp / weak / throbbing

triggers
(what made me happy, stressed etc.)

good things that happened

things that sucked

self-care

overall mood today:

DAILY CHECK-IN, PLANNER, AND TRACKER

DATE: M T W T F S S Month: __________ Day: __________

today's intention

today's challenges

wake time: ______ a.m. bedtime: ______ p.m.

hours slept: ______

how rested i feel:

micro goals	priorities	optional

medication tracker	6am-10 am	10am-2pm	2pm-6pm	6pm-10pm	overnight
	additional:				

meal tracker

time	what i ate	how i felt

caffeine	
alcohol	
nicotine/vape	

physical activity

ostomy output tracker

bag changes										
bag empty/output	l s t	l s t	l s t	l s t	l s t	l s t	l s t	l s t	l s t	l s t
bag burp										

l = liquid output / s = semi-liquid/semi-thick / t = thick

symptom tracker

pain										
stress										
fatigue										
brain fog										
scale	1	2	3	4	5	6	7	8	9	10

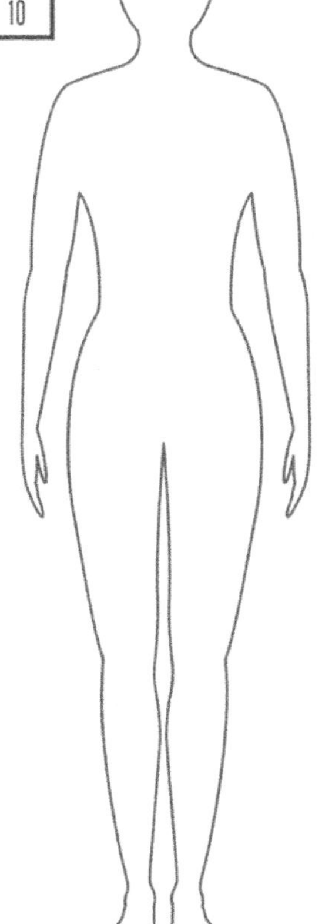

pain triggers

depression / anxiety / stress / no meds/ poor sleep / lack of activity / weather / overdid it

pain type and location:

achy / burning / stabbing / cramping / shooting / heavy / sharp / weak / throbbing

triggers
(what made me happy, stressed etc.)

good things that happened

things that sucked

self-care

overall mood today:

DAILY CHECK-IN, PLANNER, AND TRACKER

DATE: M T W T F S S Month: __________ Day: __________

today's intention

today's challenges

wake time: ______ a.m. bedtime: ______ p.m.

hours slept: ______

how rested i feel:

micro goals	priorities	optional

medication tracker	6am-10 am	10am-2pm	2pm-6pm	6pm-10pm	overnight
	additional:				

meal tracker

time	what i ate	how i felt

caffeine	
alcohol	
nicotine/vape	

physical activity

ostomy output tracker

bag changes										
bag empty/output	l s t	l s t	l s t	l s t	l s t	l s t	l s t	l s t	l s t	l s t
bag burp										

l = liquid output / s = semi-liquid/semi-thick / t = thick

symptom tracker

pain										
stress										
fatigue										
brain fog										
scale	1	2	3	4	5	6	7	8	9	10

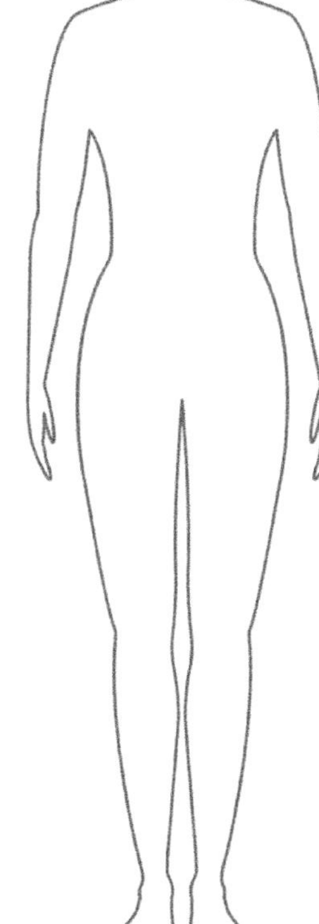

pain triggers

depression / anxiety / stress / no meds/ poor sleep / lack of activity / weather / overdid it

pain type and location:

achy / burning / stabbing / cramping / shooting / heavy / sharp / weak / throbbing

triggers (what made me happy, stressed etc.)	good things that happened	things that sucked

self-care

overall mood today:

DAILY CHECK-IN, PLANNER, AND TRACKER

DATE: M T W T F S S Month: __________ Day: __________

today's intention

today's challenges

wake time: ______ a.m. bedtime: ______ p.m.

hours slept: ______

how rested i feel:

😄 🙂 😕 ☹️ 😵

micro goals	priorities	optional

medication tracker	6am-10 am	10am-2pm	2pm-6pm	6pm-10pm	overnight
	additional:				

meal tracker

time	what i ate	how i felt

caffeine	
alcohol	
nicotine/vape	

physical activity

ostomy output tracker

bag changes										
bag empty/output	l s t	l s t	l s t	l s t	l s t	l s t	l s t	l s t	l s t	l s t
bag burp										

l = liquid output / s = semi-liquid/semi-thick / t = thick

symptom tracker

pain										
stress										
fatigue										
brain fog										
scale	1	2	3	4	5	6	7	8	9	10

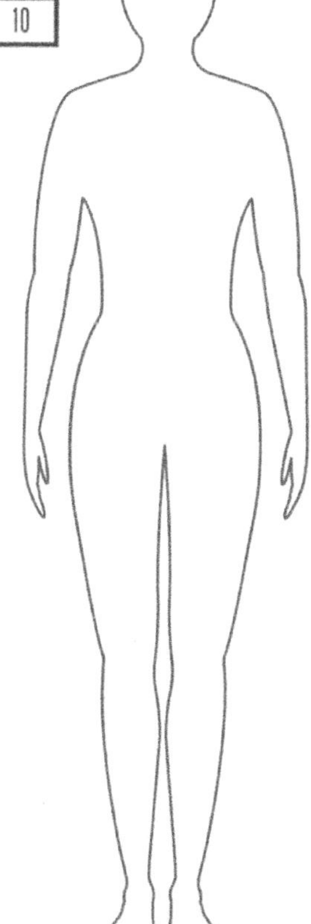

pain triggers

depression / anxiety / stress / no meds/ poor sleep / lack of activity / weather / overdid it

pain type and location:

achy / burning / stabbing / cramping / shooting / heavy / sharp / weak / throbbing

triggers
(what made me happy, stressed etc.)

good things that happened

things that sucked

self-care

overall mood today:

weekly review

week of: ____________________

my successes:

what i accepted:

what i let go:

what i did for self-care:

what was better this week:

what was worse this week:

pain summary:

medication/
care changes:

weekly planner

week of: ____________

what i will do for self-care:

what i'm looking forward to most:

what i have to get through:

how i will cope:

what i want to accomplish this week:

DAILY CHECK-IN, PLANNER, AND TRACKER

DATE: M T W T F S S Month: ___________ Day: ___________

today's intention

today's challenges

wake time: _______ a.m. bedtime: _______ p.m.

hours slept: _______

how rested i feel:

micro goals

priorities

optional

medication tracker	6am-10 am	10am-2pm	2pm-6pm	6pm-10pm	overnight
	additional:				

meal tracker

time	what i ate	how i felt

caffeine	
alcohol	
nicotine/vape	

physical activity

ostomy output tracker

bag changes										
bag empty/output	l s t	l s t	l s t	l s t	l s t	l s t	l s t	l s t	l s t	l s t
bag burp										

l = liquid output / s = semi-liquid/semi-thick / t = thick

symptom tracker

pain										
stress										
fatigue										
brain fog										
scale	1	2	3	4	5	6	7	8	9	10

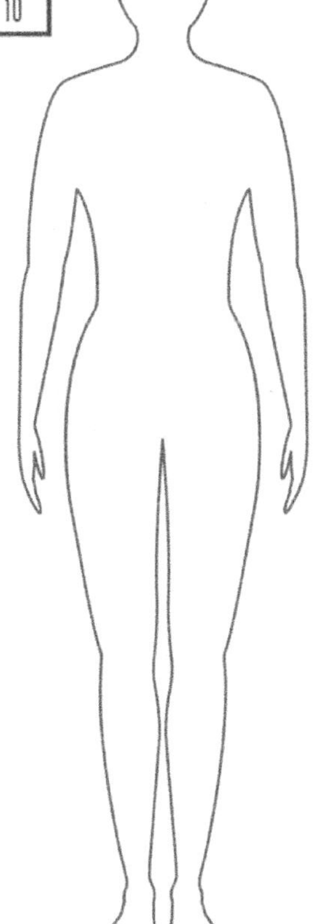

pain triggers

depression / anxiety / stress / no meds/ poor sleep / lack of activity / weather / overdid it

pain type and location:

achy / burning / stabbing / cramping / shooting / heavy / sharp / weak / throbbing

triggers (what made me happy, stressed etc.)	good things that happened	things that sucked

self-care

overall mood today:

DAILY CHECK-IN, PLANNER, AND TRACKER

DATE: M T W T F S S Month: ___________ Day: ___________

today's intention

today's challenges

wake time: _______ a.m. bedtime: _______ p.m.

hours slept: _______

how rested i feel:

😄 😊 😕 ☹️ 😵

micro goals	priorities	optional

medication tracker	6am-10 am	10am-2pm	2pm-6pm	6pm-10pm	overnight
	additional:				

meal tracker

time	what i ate	how i felt

caffeine	
alcohol	
nicotine/vape	

physical activity

ostomy output tracker

bag changes										
bag empty/output	l s t	l s t	l s t	l s t	l s t	l s t	l s t	l s t	l s t	l s t
bag burp										

l = liquid output / s = semi-liquid/semi-thick / t = thick

symptom tracker

pain										
stress										
fatigue										
brain fog										
scale	1	2	3	4	5	6	7	8	9	10

pain triggers

depression / anxiety / stress / no meds/ poor sleep / lack of activity / weather / overdid it

pain type and location:

achy / burning / stabbing / cramping / shooting / heavy / sharp / weak / throbbing

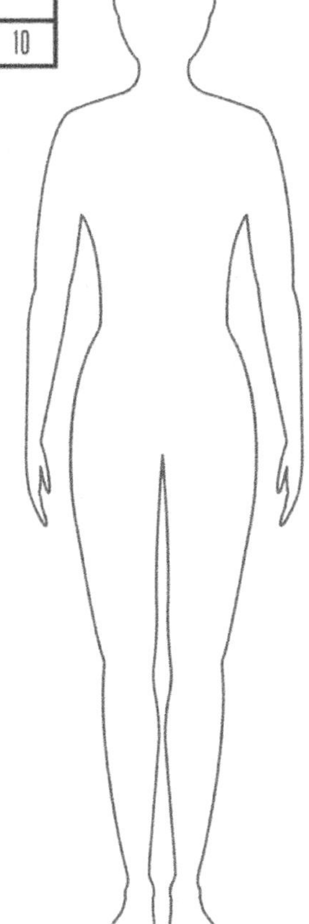

triggers
(what made me happy, stressed etc.)

good things that happened

things that sucked

self-care

overall mood today:

DAILY CHECK-IN, PLANNER, AND TRACKER

DATE: M T W T F S S Month: __________ Day: __________

today's intention

today's challenges

wake time: ______ a.m. bedtime: ______ p.m.

hours slept: ______

how rested i feel:

micro goals	priorities	optional

medication tracker	6am-10 am	10am-2pm	2pm-6pm	6pm-10pm	overnight
	additional:				

meal tracker

time	what i ate	how i felt

caffeine	
alcohol	
nicotine/vape	

physical activity

ostomy output tracker

bag changes										
bag empty/output	l s t	l s t	l s t	l s t	l s t	l s t	l s t	l s t	l s t	l s t
bag burp										

l = liquid output / s = semi-liquid/semi-thick / t = thick

symptom tracker

pain										
stress										
fatigue										
brain fog										
scale	1	2	3	4	5	6	7	8	9	10

pain triggers

depression / anxiety / stress / no meds/ poor sleep / lack of activity / weather / overdid it

pain type and location:

achy / burning / stabbing / cramping / shooting / heavy / sharp / weak / throbbing

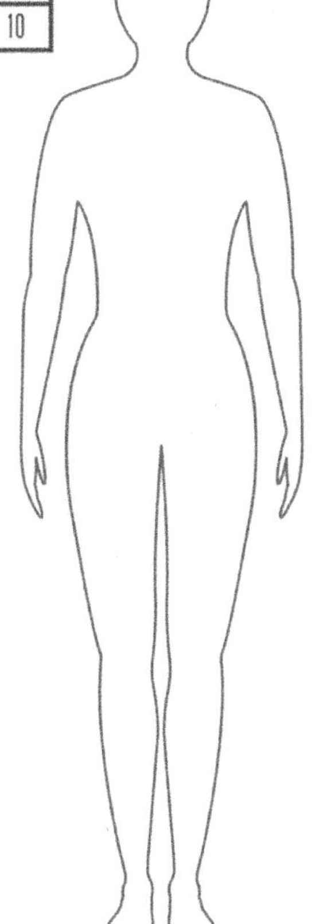

triggers
(what made me happy, stressed etc.)

good things that happened

things that sucked

self-care

overall mood today:

DAILY CHECK-IN, PLANNER, AND TRACKER

DATE: M T W T F S S Month: ____________ Day: ____________

today's intention

today's challenges

wake time: ______ a.m. bedtime: ______ p.m.

hours slept: ______

how rested i feel:

micro goals

priorities

optional

medication tracker	6am-10 am	10am-2pm	2pm-6pm	6pm-10pm	overnight
	additional:				

meal tracker

time	what i ate	how i felt

caffeine	
alcohol	
nicotine/vape	

physical activity

ostomy output tracker

bag changes										
bag empty/output	l s t	l s t	l s t	l s t	l s t	l s t	l s t	l s t	l s t	l s t
bag burp										

l = liquid output / s = semi-liquid/semi-thick / t = thick

symptom tracker

pain										
stress										
fatigue										
brain fog										
scale	1	2	3	4	5	6	7	8	9	10

pain triggers

depression / anxiety / stress / no meds/ poor sleep / lack of activity / weather / overdid it

pain type and location:

achy / burning / stabbing / cramping / shooting / heavy / sharp / weak / throbbing

triggers (what made me happy, stressed etc.)	good things that happened	things that sucked

self-care

DAILY CHECK-IN, PLANNER, AND TRACKER

DATE: M T W T F S S Month: __________ Day: __________

today's intention

today's challenges

wake time: _______ a.m. bedtime: _______ p.m.

hours slept: _______

how rested i feel:

micro goals	priorities	optional

medication tracker	6am-10 am	10am-2pm	2pm-6pm	6pm-10pm	overnight
	additional:				

meal tracker

time	what i ate	how i felt

caffeine	
alcohol	
nicotine/vape	

physical activity

ostomy output tracker

bag changes										
bag empty/output	l s t	l s t	l s t	l s t	l s t	l s t	l s t	l s t	l s t	l s t
bag burp										

l = liquid output / s = semi-liquid/semi-thick / t = thick

symptom tracker

pain										
stress										
fatigue										
brain fog										
scale	1	2	3	4	5	6	7	8	9	10

pain triggers

depression / anxiety / stress / no meds/ poor sleep / lack of activity / weather / overdid it

pain type and location:

achy / burning / stabbing / cramping / shooting / heavy / sharp / weak / throbbing

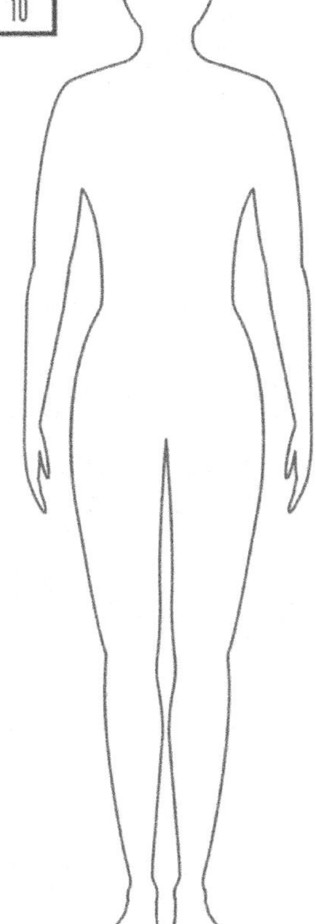

triggers
(what made me happy, stressed etc.)

good things that happened

things that sucked

self-care

overall mood today:

DAILY CHECK-IN, PLANNER, AND TRACKER

DATE: M T W T F S S Month: ___________ Day: ___________

today's intention

today's challenges

wake time: ______ a.m. bedtime: ______ p.m.

hours slept: ______

how rested i feel:

micro goals

priorities

optional

medication tracker	6am-10 am	10am-2pm	2pm-6pm	6pm-10pm	overnight
	additional:				

meal tracker

time	what i ate	how i felt

caffeine	
alcohol	
nicotine/vape	

physical activity

ostomy output tracker

bag changes										
bag empty/output	l s t	l s t	l s t	l s t	l s t	l s t	l s t	l s t	l s t	l s t
bag burp										

l = liquid output / s = semi-liquid/semi-thick / t = thick

symptom tracker

pain										
stress										
fatigue										
brain fog										
scale	1	2	3	4	5	6	7	8	9	10

pain triggers

depression / anxiety / stress / no meds/ poor sleep / lack of activity / weather / overdid it

pain type and location:

achy / burning / stabbing / cramping / shooting / heavy / sharp / weak / throbbing

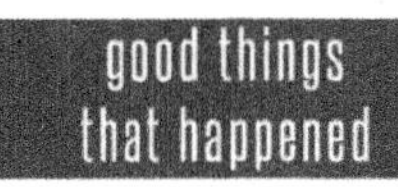

triggers
(what made me happy, stressed etc.)

good things that happened

things that sucked

self-care

overall mood today:

DAILY CHECK-IN, PLANNER, AND TRACKER

DATE: M T W T F S S Month: __________ Day: __________

today's intention

today's challenges

wake time: ______ a.m. bedtime: ______ p.m.

hours slept: ______

how rested i feel:

micro goals

priorities

optional

medication tracker	6am-10 am	10am-2pm	2pm-6pm	6pm-10pm	overnight
	additional:				

meal tracker

time	what i ate	how i felt

caffeine	
alcohol	
nicotine/vape	

physical activity

ostomy output tracker

bag changes										
bag empty/output	l s t	l s t	l s t	l s t	l s t	l s t	l s t	l s t	l s t	l s t
bag burp										

l = liquid output / s = semi-liquid/semi-thick / t = thick

symptom tracker

pain										
stress										
fatigue										
brain fog										
scale	1	2	3	4	5	6	7	8	9	10

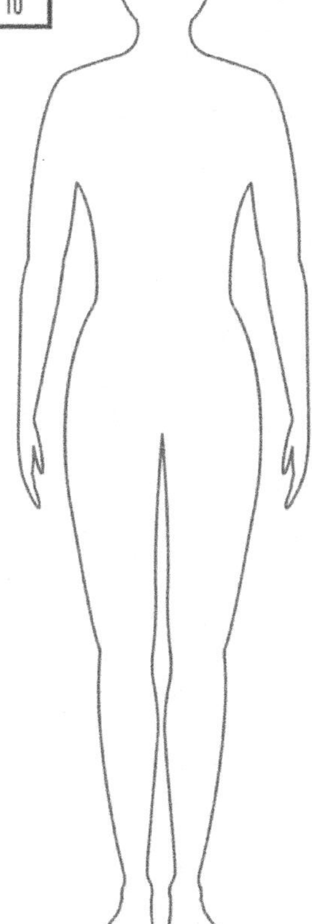

pain triggers

depression / anxiety / stress / no meds/ poor sleep / lack of activity / weather / overdid it

pain type and location:

achy / burning / stabbing / cramping / shooting / heavy / sharp / weak / throbbing

triggers
(what made me happy, stressed etc.)

good things that happened

things that sucked

self-care

overall mood today:

weekly review

week of: ____________________

my successes:

what i accepted:

what i let go:

what i did for self-care:

what was better this week:

what was worse this week:

pain summary:

medication/
care changes:

weekly planner

week of: ______________

what i will do for self-care:

what i'm looking forward to most:

what i have to get through:

how i will cope:

what i want to accomplish this week:

DAILY CHECK-IN, PLANNER, AND TRACKER

DATE: M T W T F S S Month: __________ Day: __________

today's intention

today's challenges

wake time: ______ a.m. bedtime: ______ p.m.

hours slept: ______

how rested i feel:

micro goals	priorities	optional

medication tracker	6am-10 am	10am-2pm	2pm-6pm	6pm-10pm	overnight
	additional:				

meal tracker

time	what i ate	how i felt

caffeine	
alcohol	
nicotine/vape	

physical activity

ostomy output tracker

bag changes										
bag empty/output	l s t	l s t	l s t	l s t	l s t	l s t	l s t	l s t	l s t	l s t
bag burp										

l = liquid output / s = semi-liquid/semi-thick / t = thick

symptom tracker

pain										
stress										
fatigue										
brain fog										
scale	1	2	3	4	5	6	7	8	9	10

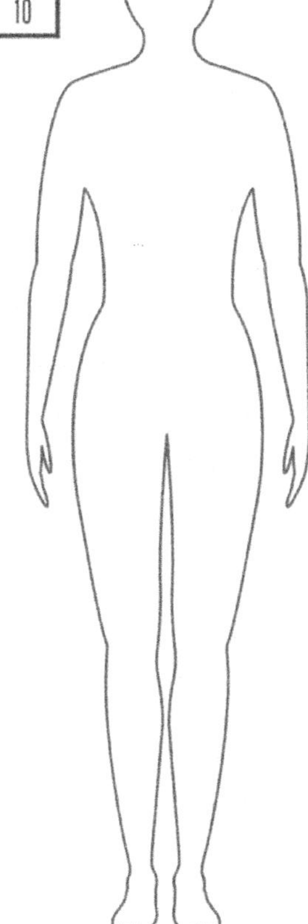

pain triggers

depression / anxiety / stress / no meds/ poor sleep / lack of activity / weather / overdid it

pain type and location:

achy / burning / stabbing / cramping / shooting / heavy / sharp / weak / throbbing

triggers
(what made me happy, stressed etc.)

good things that happened

things that sucked

self-care

overall mood today:

DAILY CHECK-IN, PLANNER, AND TRACKER

DATE: M T W T F S S Month: ___________ Day: ___________

today's intention

today's challenges

wake time: ______ a.m. bedtime: ______ p.m.

hours slept: ______

how rested i feel:

micro goals	priorities	optional

medication tracker	6am-10 am	10am-2pm	2pm-6pm	6pm-10pm	overnight
	additional:				

meal tracker

time	what i ate	how i felt

caffeine	
alcohol	
nicotine/vape	

physical activity

ostomy output tracker

bag changes										
bag empty/output	l s t	l s t	l s t	l s t	l s t	l s t	l s t	l s t	l s t	l s t
bag burp										

l = liquid output / s = semi-liquid/semi-thick / t = thick

symptom tracker

pain										
stress										
fatigue										
brain fog										
scale	1	2	3	4	5	6	7	8	9	10

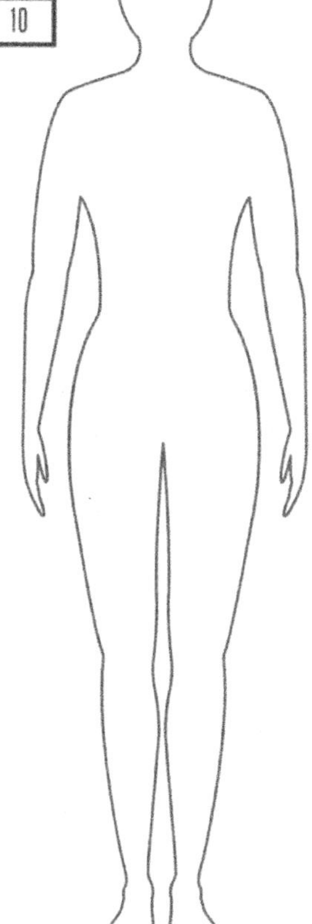

pain triggers

depression / anxiety / stress / no meds/ poor sleep / lack of activity / weather / overdid it

pain type and location:

achy / burning / stabbing / cramping / shooting / heavy / sharp / weak / throbbing

triggers
(what made me happy, stressed etc.)

good things that happened

things that sucked

self-care

overall mood today:

DAILY CHECK-IN, PLANNER, AND TRACKER

DATE: M T W T F S S Month: __________ Day: __________

today's intention

today's challenges

wake time: ______ a.m. bedtime: ______ p.m.

hours slept: ______

how rested i feel:

😄 🙂 😕 ☹️ 😵

micro goals	priorities	optional

medication tracker	6am-10 am	10am-2pm	2pm-6pm	6pm-10pm	overnight
	additional:				

meal tracker

time	what i ate	how i felt

caffeine	
alcohol	
nicotine/vape	

physical activity

ostomy output tracker

bag changes										
bag empty/output	l s t	l s t	l s t	l s t	l s t	l s t	l s t	l s t	l s t	l s t
bag burp										

l = liquid output / s = semi-liquid/semi-thick / t = thick

symptom tracker

pain										
stress										
fatigue										
brain fog										
scale	1	2	3	4	5	6	7	8	9	10

pain triggers

depression / anxiety / stress / no meds/ poor sleep / lack of activity / weather / overdid it

pain type and location:

achy / burning / stabbing / cramping / shooting / heavy / sharp / weak / throbbing

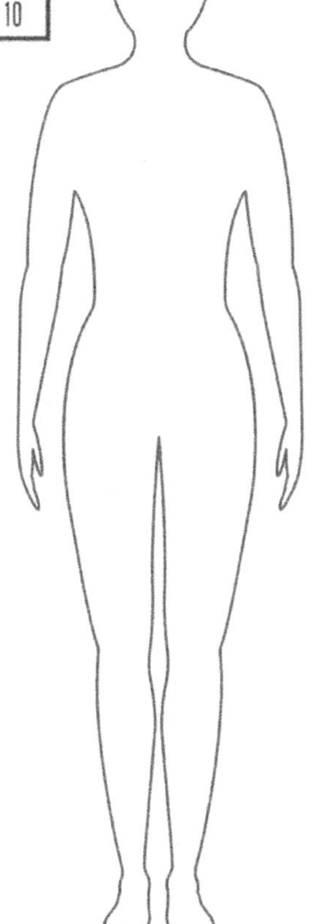

triggers
(what made me happy, stressed etc.)

good things that happened

things that sucked

self-care

overall mood today:

DAILY CHECK-IN, PLANNER, AND TRACKER

DATE: M T W T F S S Month: __________ Day: __________

today's intention

today's challenges

wake time: ______ a.m. bedtime: ______ p.m.

hours slept: ______

how rested i feel:

micro goals

priorities

optional

medication tracker	6am-10 am	10am-2pm	2pm-6pm	6pm-10pm	overnight
	additional:				

meal tracker

time	what i ate	how i felt

caffeine	
alcohol	
nicotine/vape	

physical activity

ostomy output tracker

bag changes										
bag empty/output	l s t	l s t	l s t	l s t	l s t	l s t	l s t	l s t	l s t	l s t
bag burp										

l = liquid output / s = semi-liquid/semi-thick / t = thick

symptom tracker

pain										
stress										
fatigue										
brain fog										
scale	1	2	3	4	5	6	7	8	9	10

pain triggers

depression / anxiety / stress / no meds/ poor sleep / lack of activity / weather / overdid it

pain type and location:

achy / burning / stabbing / cramping / shooting / heavy / sharp / weak / throbbing

triggers
(what made me happy, stressed etc.)

good things that happened

things that sucked

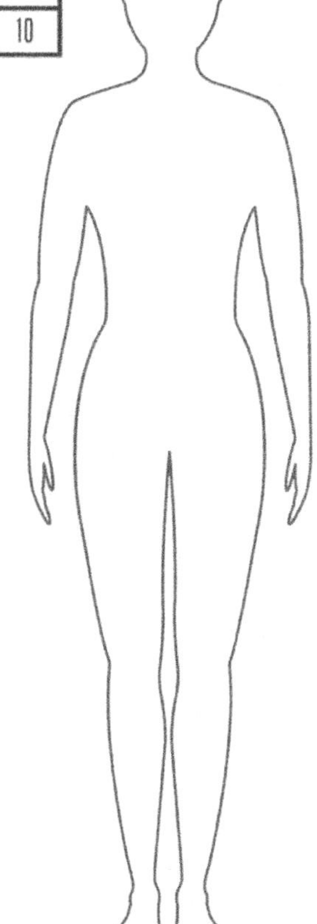

self-care

overall mood today:

DAILY CHECK-IN, PLANNER, AND TRACKER

DATE: M T W T F S S Month: __________ Day: __________

today's intention

today's challenges

wake time: ______ a.m. bedtime: ______ p.m.

hours slept: ______

how rested i feel:

😄 🙂 😕 ☹️ 😵

micro goals	priorities	optional

medication tracker	6am-10 am	10am-2pm	2pm-6pm	6pm-10pm	overnight
	additional:				

meal tracker

time	what i ate	how i felt

caffeine	
alcohol	
nicotine/vape	

physical activity

ostomy output tracker

bag changes										
bag empty/output	l s t	l s t	l s t	l s t	l s t	l s t	l s t	l s t	l s t	l s t
bag burp										

l = liquid output / s = semi-liquid/semi-thick / t = thick

symptom tracker

pain										
stress										
fatigue										
brain fog										
scale	1	2	3	4	5	6	7	8	9	10

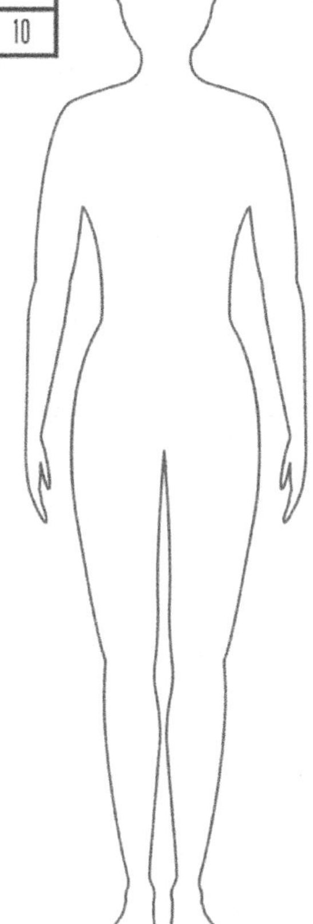

pain triggers

depression / anxiety / stress / no meds/ poor sleep / lack of activity / weather / overdid it

pain type and location:

achy / burning / stabbing / cramping / shooting / heavy / sharp / weak / throbbing

triggers
(what made me happy, stressed etc.)

good things that happened

things that sucked

self-care

overall mood today:

DAILY CHECK-IN, PLANNER, AND TRACKER

DATE: M T W T F S S Month: ___________ Day: ___________

today's intention

today's challenges

wake time: _______ a.m. bedtime: _______ p.m.

hours slept: _______

how rested i feel:

micro goals

priorities

optional

medication tracker	6am-10 am	10am-2pm	2pm-6pm	6pm-10pm	overnight
	additional:				

meal tracker

time	what i ate	how i felt

caffeine	
alcohol	
nicotine/vape	

physical activity

ostomy output tracker

bag changes										
bag empty/output	l s t	l s t	l s t	l s t	l s t	l s t	l s t	l s t	l s t	l s t
bag burp										

l = liquid output / s = semi-liquid/semi-thick / t = thick

symptom tracker

pain										
stress										
fatigue										
brain fog										
scale	1	2	3	4	5	6	7	8	9	10

pain triggers

depression / anxiety / stress / no meds/ poor sleep / lack of activity / weather / overdid it

pain type and location:

achy / burning / stabbing / cramping / shooting / heavy / sharp / weak / throbbing

triggers (what made me happy, stressed etc.)	good things that happened	things that sucked

self-care

overall mood today:

DAILY CHECK-IN, PLANNER, AND TRACKER

DATE: M T W T F S S Month: __________ Day: __________

today's intention

today's challenges

wake time: ______ a.m. bedtime: ______ p.m.

hours slept: ______

how rested i feel:

micro goals	priorities	optional

medication tracker	6am-10 am	10am-2pm	2pm-6pm	6pm-10pm	overnight
	additional:				

meal tracker

time	what i ate	how i felt

caffeine	
alcohol	
nicotine/vape	

physical activity

ostomy output tracker

bag changes										
bag empty/output	l s t	l s t	l s t	l s t	l s t	l s t	l s t	l s t	l s t	l s t
bag burp										

l = liquid output / s = semi-liquid/semi-thick / t = thick

symptom tracker

pain										
stress										
fatigue										
brain fog										
scale	1	2	3	4	5	6	7	8	9	10

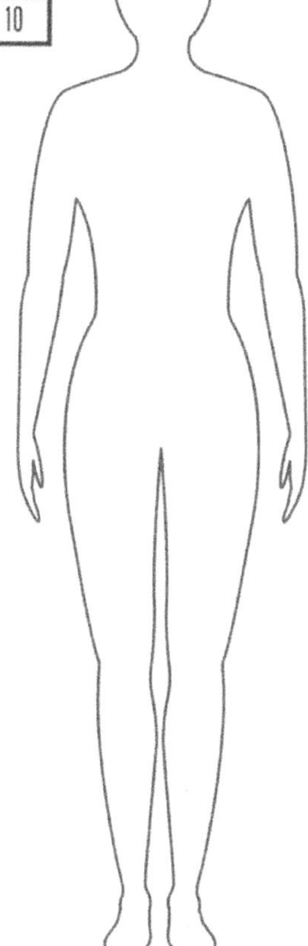

pain triggers

depression / anxiety / stress / no meds/ poor sleep / lack of activity / weather / overdid it

pain type and location:

achy / burning / stabbing / cramping / shooting / heavy / sharp / weak / throbbing

triggers
(what made me happy, stressed etc.)

good things that happened

things that sucked

self-care

overall mood today:

weekly review

week of: ____________________

my successes:

what i accepted:

what i let go:

what i did for self-care:

what was better this week:

what was worse this week:

pain summary:

medication/
care changes:

weekly planner

week of: ______________

what i will do for self-care:

what i'm looking forward to most:

what i have to get through:

how i will cope:

what i want to accomplish this week:

DAILY CHECK-IN, PLANNER, AND TRACKER

DATE: M T W T F S S Month: __________ Day: __________

today's intention

today's challenges

wake time: ______ a.m. bedtime: ______ p.m.

hours slept: ______

how rested i feel:

micro goals

priorities

optional

medication tracker	6am-10 am	10am-2pm	2pm-6pm	6pm-10pm	overnight
	additional:				

meal tracker

time	what i ate	how i felt

caffeine	
alcohol	
nicotine/vape	

physical activity

ostomy output tracker

bag changes										
bag empty/output	l s t	l s t	l s t	l s t	l s t	l s t	l s t	l s t	l s t	l s t
bag burp										

l = liquid output / s = semi-liquid/semi-thick / t = thick

symptom tracker

pain										
stress										
fatigue										
brain fog										
scale	1	2	3	4	5	6	7	8	9	10

pain triggers

depression / anxiety / stress / no meds/ poor sleep / lack of activity / weather / overdid it

pain type and location:

achy / burning / stabbing / cramping / shooting / heavy / sharp / weak / throbbing

triggers
(what made me happy, stressed etc.)

good things that happened

things that sucked

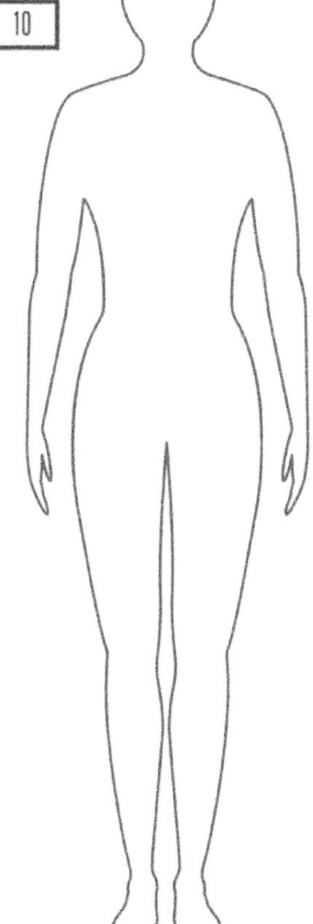

self-care

overall mood today:

DAILY CHECK-IN, PLANNER, AND TRACKER

DATE: M T W T F S S Month: ____________ Day: ____________

today's intention

today's challenges

wake time: ______ a.m. bedtime: ______ p.m.

hours slept: ______

how rested i feel:

micro goals

priorities

optional

medication tracker	6am-10 am	10am-2pm	2pm-6pm	6pm-10pm	overnight
	additional:				

meal tracker

time	what i ate	how i felt

caffeine	
alcohol	
nicotine/vape	

physical activity

ostomy output tracker

bag changes										
bag empty/output	l s t	l s t	l s t	l s t	l s t	l s t	l s t	l s t	l s t	l s t
bag burp										

l = liquid output / s = semi-liquid/semi-thick / t = thick

symptom tracker

pain										
stress										
fatigue										
brain fog										
scale	1	2	3	4	5	6	7	8	9	10

pain triggers

depression / anxiety / stress / no meds/ poor sleep / lack of activity / weather / overdid it

pain type and location:

achy / burning / stabbing / cramping / shooting / heavy / sharp / weak / throbbing

triggers
(what made me happy, stressed etc.)

good things that happened

things that sucked

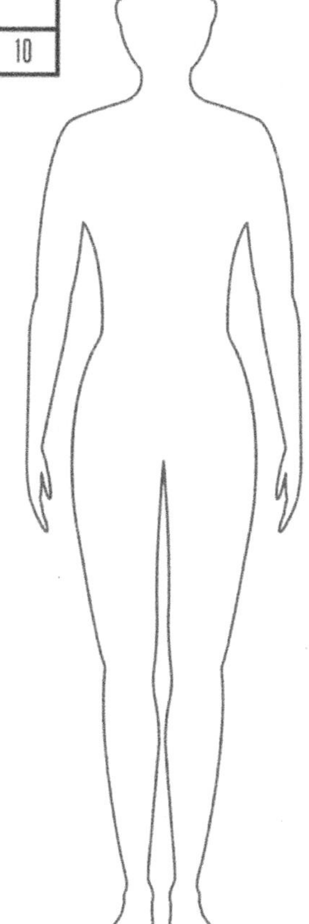

self-care

overall mood today:

DAILY CHECK-IN, PLANNER, AND TRACKER

DATE: M T W T F S S Month: __________ Day: __________

today's intention

today's challenges

wake time: ______ a.m. bedtime: ______ p.m.

hours slept: ______

how rested i feel:

micro goals	priorities	optional

medication tracker	6am-10 am	10am-2pm	2pm-6pm	6pm-10pm	overnight
	additional:				

meal tracker

time	what i ate	how i felt

caffeine	
alcohol	
nicotine/vape	

physical activity

ostomy output tracker

bag changes										
bag empty/output	l s t	l s t	l s t	l s t	l s t	l s t	l s t	l s t	l s t	l s t
bag burp										

l = liquid output / s = semi-liquid/semi-thick / t = thick

symptom tracker

pain										
stress										
fatigue										
brain fog										
scale	1	2	3	4	5	6	7	8	9	10

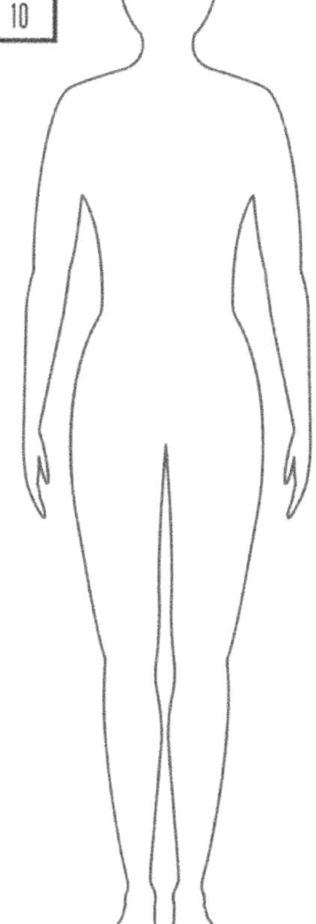

pain triggers

depression / anxiety / stress / no meds/ poor sleep / lack of activity / weather / overdid it

pain type and location:

achy / burning / stabbing / cramping / shooting / heavy / sharp / weak / throbbing

triggers
(what made me happy, stressed etc.)

good things that happened

things that sucked

self-care

overall mood today:

weekly review

week of: ____________________

my successes:

what i accepted:

what i let go:

what i did for self-care:

what was better this week:

what was worse this week:

pain summary:

medication/
care changes:

monthly review

month: ______________

my successes:

what i accepted:

what i let go:

what i did for self-care:

what was better this month:

what was worse this month:

pain summary:

medication/
care changes:

notes:

ostomy product tracker

product	company	product #	serial #	cost	source	refill date

notes:

ostomy supply trial tracker

product: ______________ company: ________________ cost: _______
pros:

cons:

overall rating: ☆☆☆☆☆

product: ______________ company: ________________ cost: _______
pros:

cons:

overall rating: ☆☆☆☆☆

product: ______________ company: ________________ cost: _______
pros:

cons:

overall rating: ☆☆☆☆☆

product: ______________ company: ________________ cost: _______
pros:

cons:

overall rating: ☆☆☆☆☆

ostomy supply trial tracker

product: ______________ company: ______________ cost: ________
pros:

cons:

overall rating: ☆☆☆☆☆

product: ______________ company: ______________ cost: ________
pros:

cons:

overall rating: ☆☆☆☆☆

product: ______________ company: ______________ cost: ________
pros:

cons:

overall rating: ☆☆☆☆☆

product: ______________ company: ______________ cost: ________
pros:

cons:

overall rating: ☆☆☆☆☆

stoma wound tracker

location

start date: ________

type of wound/irritation: ________________________

symptoms: ________________________

cause: ________________________

treatment: ________________________

healed by date: ________________________

location

start date: ________

type of wound/irritation: ________________________

symptoms: ________________________

cause: ________________________

treatment: ________________________

healed by date: ________________________

location

start date: ________

type of wound/irritation: ________________________

symptoms: ________________________

cause: ________________________

treatment: ________________________

healed by date: ________________________

location

start date: ________

type of wound/irritation: ________________________

symptoms: ________________________

cause: ________________________

treatment: ________________________

healed by date: ________________________

stoma wound tracker

location

start date: __________

type of wound/irritation: ______________________________

symptoms: ______________________________

cause: ______________________________

treatment: ______________________________

healed by date: ______________________________

location

start date: __________

type of wound/irritation: ______________________________

symptoms: ______________________________

cause: ______________________________

treatment: ______________________________

healed by date: ______________________________

location

start date: __________

type of wound/irritation: ______________________________

symptoms: ______________________________

cause: ______________________________

treatment: ______________________________

healed by date: ______________________________

location

start date: __________

type of wound/irritation: ______________________________

symptoms: ______________________________

cause: ______________________________

treatment: ______________________________

healed by date: ______________________________

trigger tracker

trigger	result/symptoms	how i can avoid	how i can cope

period tracker

start date:
flow: spotting / light / medium / heavy
effect on symptoms:
what helps:
end date:

pain										
stress										
fatigue										
brain fog										
scale	1	2	3	4	5	6	7	8	9	10

start date:
flow: spotting / light / medium / heavy
effect on symptoms:
what helps:
end date:

pain										
stress										
fatigue										
brain fog										
scale	1	2	3	4	5	6	7	8	9	10

start date:
flow: spotting / light / medium / heavy
effect on symptoms:
what helps:
end date:

pain										
stress										
fatigue										
brain fog										
scale	1	2	3	4	5	6	7	8	9	10

start date:
flow: spotting / light / medium / heavy
effect on symptoms:
what helps:
end date:

pain										
stress										
fatigue										
brain fog										
scale	1	2	3	4	5	6	7	8	9	10

start date:
flow: spotting / light / medium / heavy
effect on symptoms:
what helps:
end date:

pain										
stress										
fatigue										
brain fog										
scale	1	2	3	4	5	6	7	8	9	10

Comments or suggestions? Let us know
at gloryboxpress@gmail.com!

Made in the USA
Las Vegas, NV
02 April 2022